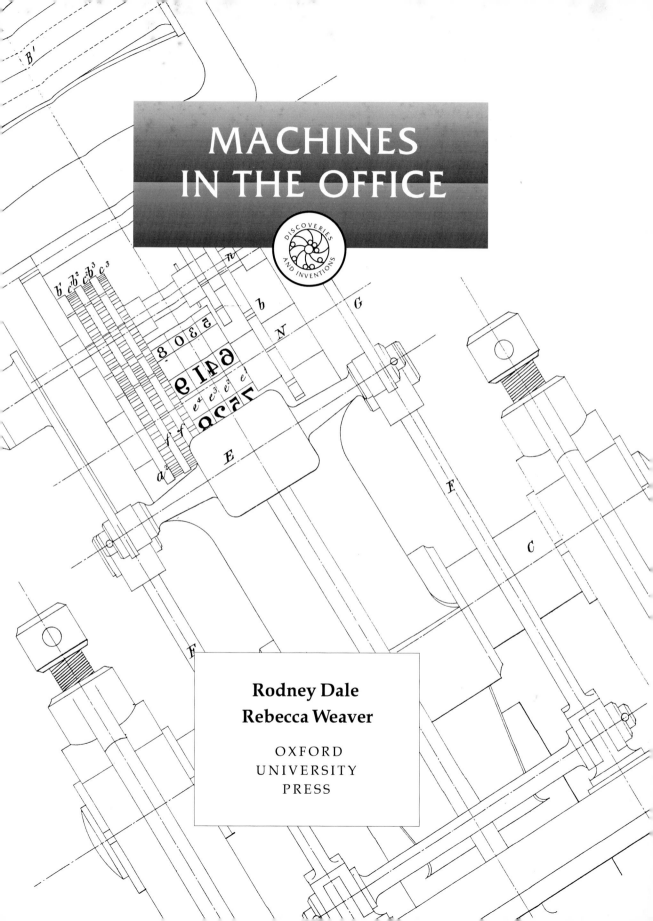

MACHINES
IN THE OFFICE

DISCOVERIES
AND INVENTIONS

Rodney Dale
Rebecca Weaver

OXFORD
UNIVERSITY
PRESS

Page 1

Detail from British patent no 13,063 of 1850, Baranowski's machinery for counting, numbering and labelling.

Pages 2 and 3

A typewriting department in the 1920s.

Photographic acknowledgements

All illustrations in this book have been taken from out-of-copyright material in The British Library's collections with the exception of those which carry a credit line in the accompanying caption. Patents are numbered and dated for ease of reference.
The authors would like to thank David Gestetner for his help.

OXFORD UNIVERSITY PRESS

Oxford New York Toronto
Delhi Bombay Calcutta Madras Karachi
Kuala Lumpur Singapore Hong Kong Tokyo
Nairobi Dar es Salaam Cape Town
Melbourne Auckland Madrid
and associated companies in
Berlin Ibadan

First published in 1993 by The British Library. First published in North and South America by Oxford University Press, Inc.,
200 Madison Avenue, New York, New York 10016 by arrangement with The British Library.

Oxford is a registered trademark of Oxford University Press

Library of Congress Cataloging in Publication Data

Dale, Rodney
  Machines in the office / Rodney Dale and Rebecca Weaver.
    p.64, 24.6 x 18.9 cm — (Discoveries and Inventions)
  Includes bibliographical references and index.
  Summary: Explores some of the discoveries and inventions that have improved working conditions in offices, from the fountain pen to the telephone.
  ISBN 0-19-521000-X. — ISBN 0-19-521004-2 (pbk.)
  1. Office equipment and supplies — History — Juvenile literature. [1. Office equipment and supplies — History.] I. Weaver, Rebecca. II. Title. III. Series.
HF5548.D2 1993   93-15314
651'.2'09 — dc20   CIP
                                              AC

Designed by Roger Davies.
Set in Palatino on Ventura.
Printed in Italy.

Contents

Introduction

This book could well be subtitled 'Edison – Office Hero'. The influence of the American inventor Thomas Alva Edison (1847–1931) on the transformation of the office is outstanding. Changes would undoubtedly have come – the time was right, and his name may not always be the first one commonly associated with them – but somewhere along the line, his inventiveness is paramount. He contributed to the telegraph, telephone, teleprinter, typewriter, Dictaphone, the copying machine (though he sold off his rights almost as soon as he had them) and last, but not least, the electric light bulb, which probably did more than anything to improve working conditions for the many thousands of office workers required to toil away in dingy quarters ill suited to the amount of machinery they came to house.

Discoveries and inventions are made by and for people. Before we explore some of the inventive effort poured into the office, let us look at the people and the conditions in which they laboured.

What is an office? 'Office' for long referred to the position and related duties rather than the place where the 'officer' spent his time. As time went on and the amount of business attached to the post grew, the word became synonymous with the place where clerical, administrative or accounting transactions were carried out. Large estates, both secular and monastic, were run from offices by a 'reeve', steward, or clerk. Merchants had clerks to keep accounts and look after orders. The legal service, both royal and baronial, and parliament also needed to keep records of what was going on. So, from the outset, clerks and officers have been pen-pushers, keepers of records, purveyors of information. This book is the story of the technology they acquired, the better to handle their information.

Many of our received perceptions of the 19th-century office come from our reading of fiction. From Charles Dickens (1812–70), for example, we have the well-known relationship between Ebenezer Scrooge and his clerk Bob Cratchit in *A Christmas Carol*. The *Diary of a Nobody* (George and Weedon Grossmith, 1892), the serialized diary of Mr Charles Pooter, a City clerk, affords many humorous insights into life both at home and at the office. We learn, for example, of the petty one-upmanship that occurs in sedentary places of work, foreshadowing the imagined snubs of a later date – being given the 'wrong' parking place, too small a desk, too small a carpet, an inferior view, and so on.

Office work is the essence of *The Job* by Sinclair Lewis (1926), and crops up in *USA* by John Dos Passos (1930). JB Priestley's *Angel Pavement* (1930) is the story of the declining fortune of Mr Smeeth, an esteemed book-keeper in a small firm.

According to C Wright Mills in *White collar: the American middle classes*, by the middle of the 19th century, the standard equipment on both sides of the Atlantic in most types of office was the 'cash book, ledger, iron spike, day book, quill, letter press and box files'. The book-keeper recorded all transactions in the day book, cash book, or ledger. All current orders and memoranda were speared on the spike. Even so, as the 19th century entered its final quarter, clerks – male – became very defensive about their positions:

Anybody who can write may be a clerk: this is the general notion which is far from correct. Among other accomplishments an accurate and thorough knowledge of book-keeping is required, so is a knowledge of the style employed in official and business letters. *Chambers' Journal* 7 September 1877

That probably puts it in a nutshell. The unfortunate thing for male clerical prestige was that increasing numbers of people – including women – could fulfil those functions and those functions were metamorphosing into something slightly different.

Women in the office

The arrival of women on the scene did not pass unnoticed at the time and in no way was it discreet or selective. From *Chambers'*, September 1877, again:

Employment of females in certain departments of clerical-labour would seem to be a thing much to be desired and

A Dickensian office, illustrated by 'Phiz' in *Nicholas Nickleby.*

encouraged: and there is ample scope for such employment where the duties are light, straightforward and not too onerous in character.

The writer quotes the response to a vacancy for eleven junior counter-women at Metropolitan Post Offices as being 'one thousand to one thousand, five hundred young ladies'. Fortunately, 'this extension of female labour will by natural laws not proceed beyond natural limits' and every cloud has a silver lining even if some young men, who ought to be adopting more suitable vocations anyway are displaced – 'the accomplishments of account-keeping and a training in good business habits are calculated to make better wives and mothers.'

A disgruntled City clerk put the matter rather more directly in 1880:

While women now enter into competition in the field of mental labour which has always been considered strictly a man's province, they omit to learn how to mend a stocking, or cook a steak, both among a long string of things specially women's work, but spurned by those to whom an unhealthy education has given higher disproportionate aspirations.

Mid-Victorian feminists saw clerical work as eminently suitable for middle-class women who were anxious to make themselves independent. The 1861 census reveals a meagre 279 female clerks in Britain. By 1911, there were 124,843 female clerks; though they were only 18 per cent of all clerks employed. However, between 1861 and 1911 the overall percentage increase of female clerks was 44,646, whereas the percentage increase of male clerks was only 645.

The general education required for many clerical posts was not of a particularly high standard, but the mechanization of many functions in the office opened the field for entrepreneurial ladies – especially in America – to open business schools for women and give them a commercial education to fit them specifically for work in the newer style office. Jessie Boucherette of the Society for Promotion of the Employment of Women (SPEW) in Britain, and Mary F Seymour who founded *Business Woman's Journal* in 1889 in America, were two such women.

Business colleges were big business in America, and feature in most of the contemporary novels which have 'office women' as their central characters. 'Copying offices' and 'Typewriting offices' were established in Britain. Typists were known at this stage as 'lady type-writers' to distinguish them from the machine. By the beginning of the First World War, commercial training was open to all young girls either at school or at 'continuation classes' held in the evenings. 'A knowledge of shorthand and training is the only requisite deemed necessary to start on a career *ad Parnassum*' claimed *The Fingerpost*, published by the London Central Bureau for the Employment of Women in 1906. Whether they could reach Parnassus – the pinnacle of their profession – even if they indeed aspired to do so at this stage, is debatable. Much of the attraction for many young women was that office work was not shop work, factory work or domestic service. Although around the turn of the century some university-trained women took up clerical work, stereotypical views of female advancement prevented their rising to positions of any real eminence.

Why did employers take women on? As regards the typewriter – the machine – contemporaries likened its action to a piano; consequently it was especially suited to a woman's delicacy of touch. It was asserted that women were temperamentally more suited to routine and lack of opportunities than men; that they were more docile and easier to manage and took kindly to sedentary employment. Above all, as the Inland Revenue confessed in 1888 'they are so cheap and there is no superannuation'. The female office worker was here to stay.

Conditions in established offices were rarely conducive to the sudden arrival of a female and there were plenty of knowing women who specialized in pointing out the moral pitfalls of mixed offices. In 1890 the Board of Agriculture employed one woman. She was 'put' in a dingy basement room and there was a firm order that no male member of staff over the age of 15 was to visit her. Many establishments provided no female restrooms. Some observers considered that women raised the tone; others that work in an office was the first step on the road to prostitution. According to Alan Delgado in *The Enormous File*, when female typists entered offices in the 1890s in New York, cuspidor manufacturers began to go out of business. Fortunately *Businesswoman's Journal* gave advice on how to behave, and how to dress to become most efficient:

Never chat during business hours. Be as lady-like as you would be in a parlor. Above all avoid undue familiarity with the clerks. Never accept gifts and other attention from your employer unless he has introduced you to members of his family and you have been received as a social equity of them. Do not receive letters or social calls at your place of business. Never use the telephone for your personal business.

The development of the office

There was obviously a hierarchy in types of office, as in life itself. As new office machines became available, many large establishments – especially those engaged, for example, in manufacturing 'modern' goods – reflected their modernity by installing them. Others, smaller, with more established functions and styles –

The idle and the industrious apprentices: 'Mr Goodchild, the Industrious Apprentice, is seen pegging away at his office work, while his fellow clerk, Tom Idle, is wasting his Master's time and his own by learning during office hours a frivolous ballad which he intends to sing in the evening "in society".' The appointments in the office of 1871, seen in the pages of *Judy, or the London serio-comic journal.*

A battery of comptometers at work – in a 'figure factory', 1923.

lawyers' offices, for example – avoided any change or added expense until the eccentricity of old-fashioned ways became counterproductive.

Developments were perhaps faster in the United States, though the picture conveyed by contemporary films is not always one of great modernity. Nevertheless, the dawn of scientific management broke earlier in America than it did in Britain. The National Association of Office Managers was formed in 1919, though this as yet had less to do with machines than with those who worked them. In 1929, in one firm, 'orders are passed along by means of a belt and lights from a chief clerk to a series of checkers and typists, each of whom does one operation. The girl at the head of the line interprets the order . . . the second girl prices . . . the third girl . . . the fourth . . . the fifth time-stamps it . . .'

The office revolution did not really take off until after the Second World War. In the late 1940s, in America, about 3,000 different machines were on display at trade exhibitions. Offices resembled factories in their appearance and methods. Time-and-motion studies encouraged the reduction of personnel, and provided a statistical basis for seeking increases in output. Apparently, merely reshuffling the desk plan can effect a saving of 15 per cent in standard hour units.

Even if some organizations have invested more in machines than in people, the bond between offices and women has never broken. As the workload grew, offices became departmentalized and mechanized and women took on all functions. Nowadays it suits many women to fit some temporary office work into their lives – symptomatic of the restless freedom women have acquired for themselves after a century of struggle.

The office on the move.

Above
The typewriting office of the new Birmingham–
Broad Street express of 1910.

Right
'By means of the Yöst Typewriter the Politician, the
Business Man, the Professional Man or Private
Gentleman can conduct his Correspondence etc on a
motor trip as effectively as in his own office or at
home.' The Yöst has 'no troublesome shift key, but a
key for Every Character – simplicity itself.'

SELECTED QUESTIONS.

The following questions have been selected from actual papers, and they give an adequate notion of the scope of the examination :—

ARITHMETIC.—(Elementary): (1) Add together $7\frac{5}{42}$, $10\frac{7}{15}$, $6\frac{6}{7}$, and $\frac{8}{35}$. (2) Subtract 59·79803 from 162·702. (3) Multiply 76870 by 31·92006. (4) Calculate to the nearest penny the simple interest on £762 5s. 11d for five years at $\frac{3}{8}$ per cent. There are, also, the usual compound addition sums to be added up. Advanced : (1) Define a measure, a multiple, a common measure and a common multiple. Show that the least common multiple of any two numbers is obtained by dividing their product by their greatest common measure. The least common multiple of two numbers is 3060288 and their greatest common measure is 168. One of them is 12096 : find the other. (2) A square field has a shrub border 11 yards wide, running along all four sides, within the boundary of the field. This border contains one acre : find the area of the field. (3) Explain clearly the operation 70582 ÷ 129. Show that any number that will divide each of two numbers without remainder, will also divide their difference. (4) A man lost 3s. 4d. on the sale of a certain article at a certain price. Had that price been doubled, he would have gained half as much as he gave for the article. What would he gain if he sold it for a guinea?

HANDWRITING.—The test in handwriting consists in copying a tabular statement in half-an-hour. At one examination this statement referred to the analysis and consumption of tobacco. The Civil Service style of handwriting obtains most marks.

ORTHOGRAPHY.—There are two exercises in dictation given, each occupying half-an-hour. At one examination the most difficult words were : lassitude, disappointment, physiognomy, manor, barbarous, sweet-briar, mignonette, fatality, indispensable, replenished, irresistible, vassals.

ENGLISH COMPOSITION.—There is a choice of three subjects and not less than two pages have to be filled in an hour. The following have been given : (1) A Journey round my Garden. (2) The Heroines of Scott. (3) Method in Daily Life.

GEOGRAPHY.—About five questions have to be answered in $1\frac{1}{2}$ hours. Such are : (1) Describe with a sketch map the most important river systems of England or Scotland. Account for the crowding together of population in certain river basins. (2) On the accompanying outline map of the British Isles, mark the principal headlands and also the chief ports and six of the principal steamboat routes connecting them. (3) Starting from the meridian of Greenwich, and proceeding from east to west, name the principal places lying on or near the Tropics of Cancer and Capricorn. (4) Mention where the following rivers rise, and the seas into which they flow : Volga, Amu Daria, Hoang-ho, Lena, Mississippi, Irrawady, Indus, Euphrates, Schelde.

ENGLISH HISTORY.—The number of questions to be answered is usually six. out of from 12 to 18 questions asked. (1) Give some account of the rise of the towns, and of the growth of the power of the Commons of England. (2) How far were the successes of Elizabeth's reign due to herself, how far to her councillors, and how far to the character of her people? (3) What do you know of Sir John Eliot, Noy, Laud, and Faulkland ? (4) Give an account of the Jacobite Rebellion of 1715.

Questions 'selected from actual papers' for the Civil Service Clerks' Exam – *Phonetic Journal* 1892.

Communicating on paper

The style of writing has always depended on the writing implements and the material written upon. Early writing civilisations – Babylonian, Egyptian, Greek, Roman – all made use of fairly stiff, sharpened reeds to inscribe soft papyrus sheets, wet clay or wax tablets, and their styles of writing reveal a gradually acquired sophistication of shape – less angular, more rounded – born no doubt of increasing practice and demands on the art. (In China, writing has remained an art, with scribes using brushes.)

Account of barley issued as loans to workmen attached to various temples, and as pay to other hired men. Neo-Sumerian cuneiform script of 2048 BC.

Lord Palmerston's quill pens 'mounted in his usual mode of keeping them'.

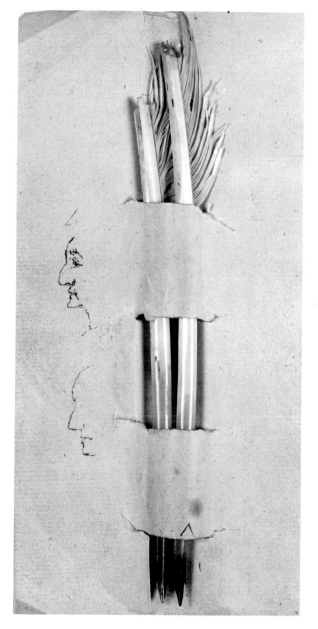

A medieval scribe using a quill pen. He is holding down the parchment with a curved penknife.

Quill pens and nibs

The quill pen (*penna* is the Latin for feather) was first used in about the 5th century. Goose, swan, peacock, turkey – even crow – feathers have all been used at one time or another. The point was cut squarish to a modern nib shape and a slit made to make it more flexible and help the ink to flow. The quill point needed frequent re-cutting and the folding pen-knife was soon developed. Later came a special device into which the end of the new quill was pushed; a special blade then performed all the operations necessary to shape it in one movement. Some quills could be fitted with a nib, made from horn or tortoiseshell and reinforced with chips of precious stones to make it last longer. These nibs can have made little impact for in 1832 (it was

said) nearly 34,000,000 quill pens were in use in Britain, most imported from Europe.

Quills are still available from certain specialised stationers, and a London bank will even provide one should it be requested. But to all intents and purposes, and despite advertisements for them as late as 1893, the quill pen went out of use once the steel nib was perfected. That took some doing; the first British patent for a metal pen was taken out by Bryan Donkin in 1808. To begin with, the nibs were inflexible, scratchy and prone to rust because of the corrosive properties of the ink. Ink was originally made with lamp black, gum and a little water. Vinegar was added to 'fix' the writing. Concurrent with the development of steel nibs were investigations into ink making, and using tannic acid and later on aniline dyes to try and prevent it

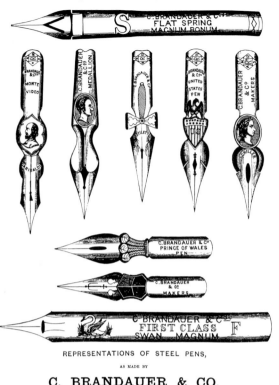

REPRESENTATIONS OF STEEL PENS,

AS MADE BY

C. BRANDAUER & CO.

Manufacturers of Steel Pens of every description,

NEW JOHN STREET PEN WORKS,

BIRMINGHAM.

(2)

corroding the nibs. The name of Henry Stephens has been associated with ink since he began manufacturing it in 1834.

The 'Regulating Spring Pen' appeared in 1843; it had a sliding spring to regulate its flexibility. About the same time Joseph Gillot patented his 'improved' nib. This coincided with the introduction in Great Britain of the penny postal service (1840), and the resultant upsurge in letter writing ensured that both nibs and post became correspondingly efficient. Many schools changed over from slates to pens and paper. Wonderfully elaborately-titled nib designs appeared, many with the heads of the famous embossed upon them: 'The Duke', 'The Gilt Flange', 'Figaro', 'International' and so on. Nib holders – what we now call the pen itself – became suitably ornate to accompany the illustrious nibs. Some nibs had five points for drawing music staves; others had three points for cash book divisions.

Fountain pens

For the prolific writer, however, there was a pressing need to have a pen which could somehow hold a measure of ink and put an end to all the dip-dipping into ink wells. Samuel Pepys (1633–1703) refers to some sort of reservoir pen in his diary; but efforts to perfect this sort of pen were clearly unsatisfactory.

One of the earliest pen patents is dated 1809, from Frederick Bartholomew Försch for 'several improvements calculated to promote the facility in writing'. In the same year, Joseph Bramah, having momentarily improved the water closet, registered a patent for a 'new method of making pens, pen-making machines, pen holders and fountain pens.' In 1819 appeared The Penographic Fountain Pen which had a cock to control the ink feed to the nib.

These pens were 'regular' fountain pens; in other words, the ink had to be poured in to the reservoir. In 1823 JJ Parker produced the first self-filler, in which a piston drew the ink up into the reservoir by suction.

Leakage was still a problem, mitigated only marginally by the accidental discovery of blotting paper. Prior to this people had sprinkled 'pounce' – powdered pumice, cuttlefish or even chalk – over their writing, kept on their desks in a pounce pot. About 1840 a papermaker forgot to add 'size' (a surface sealer) to his mixture and produced blotting paper.

In 1883 – notwithstanding his blotter – Lewis Edson Waterman, a New York insurance agent, lost a sale because of a leaky pen. Necessity being the mother of invention, he hit upon the idea of using capillary action – the molecular force which makes a liquid creep along a crack. Within three years he had perfectly harnessed the effect that is at the root of the fountain pen action today.

The stylographic pen recalled the ancient idea of writing with a pointed stylus rather than a squared-off nib. Försch and Howard had registered a patent for one in 1809. Stylographics were no better than nibbed pens for filling and not leaking. In a fictional account of 1892, we read:

[It] was simply nine-and-sixpence thrown in the mud. It has caused me constant annoyance and irritability of temper. The ink oozes out of the top, making a mess on my hands, and once at the office when I was knocking the palm of my hand on the desk to jerk the ink down, Mr Perkupp, who had just entered, called out 'Stop that knocking! I suppose that is you Mr Pitt?' ... 'No, sir: I beg pardon, it is Mr Pooter with his pen; it has been going on all the morning.'

No fewer than nine patents were filed this same year for improved stylographic pens, but it was Waterman's breakthrough which finally tamed the leaky pen.

In another account, a self-important clerk was duped by a different approach to the inky problem – the Aquapen. This appears to have contained caked ink which would run as normal ink when water, with which the pen's reservoir was filled, was in contact

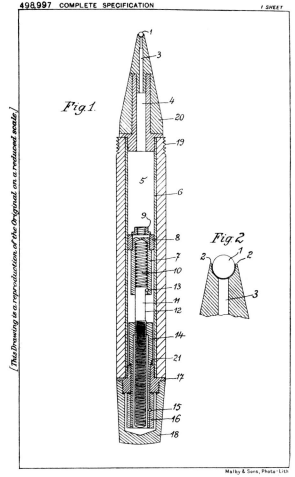

British patent no 498,997 of 1938 for Biro's ballpoint pen.

with it. There were 'fourteen different things you had to do in filling an Aquapen ... and you had to do them all in the right order. There was also a list of ten special warnings against things which you might not do ... and they were nearly all of them things you would naturally have done if you had not been warned.' Despite following the instructions to the letter our hero managed to ruin a whole set of clothes – including his braces – because the special Aquapen ink dissolved rubber as well.

The ballpoint

The ballpoint pen was another effort to improve writing appliances. A ball housed in a socket revolves

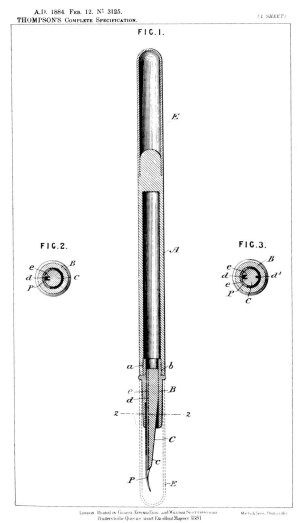

British patent no 3,125 of 1884 for Lewis E Waterman's fountain pen.

freely during writing and draws ink from the reservoir. A patent was taken out in 1888 by John Loud. The main problem this time lay in developing a suitable reservoir for a suitable ink, which had to be a great deal more viscous than fountain pen or stylographic ink. Ballpoints failed to gain credence until the Hungarian László Biro patented his first design in 1938. Though the ballpoint, or 'biro', took over, it still has to bow in the face of the more conspicuous artistry of the fountain pen.

The pencil

'Lead' pencils were originally made of pure lead, which leaves a visible trail on paper. The 'lead' of the modern pencil is made of carbon in the form of graphite, or of a graphite compound. Graphite was discovered in the mid-16th century in Borrowdale, Cumberland. As supplies began to diminish it was mixed with clay; it is the proportion of clay to graphite that determines the degree of hardness of a pencil. Once prepared, the graphite is laid in a narrow channel in a wood with good whittling properties so that the pencil can be sharpened; cedar was most often chosen. Propelling or mechanical pencils usually have finer pieces of lead advanced by a clutch or screwed in or out of the barrel.

Shorthand

If you are involved in doing a great deal of writing, especially taking notes to someone else's order, no matter what instrument you choose, longhand can be tedious. Shorthand, or at least an agreed system of abbreviations, is extremely old. A version was taught to scribes in Egypt, as it was later in Rome where it was used for recording trials and speeches in the Senate. By the 16th century in Europe, and especially Great Britain, writing had most definitely moved on from being the sole province of scribes and monks. This was a result both of the Renaissance broadening intellectual horizons and of the increase in trade and associated commerce. Tudor merchants chose to write their own letters in longhand – this being proof of identity – but a shorthand was sometimes used *eg* L = London; prt = present; lre = letter. In the 17th century both John Evelyn and Samuel Pepys used shorthand in their diaries, and commonly-agreed systems were given encouragement when Parliament in Britain permitted the re-

porting of its debates in 1772. By the time of the penny post in 1840 no fewer than eight systems were in existence.

Sir Isaac Pitman (1813–1897), who had been a clerk and elementary school master, was interested in shorthand as a teaching aid. His 'phonography' system, which he made public in 1837, used signs to represent sounds. Previous systems had used signs to represent letters. Pitman hoped his system would replace writing and so set himself up as its publicist and propagandist. As its publication virtually coincided with the introduction of the penny post, Pitman's shorthand course became the first correspondence course. Graduates of the course became members of the 'Phonetic Society', which published the *Phonetic Journal.*

Sir Edward Walkin claimed to be the first to use shorthand in business practice. As General Manager of the Manchester, Sheffield & Lincolnshire Railway in 1853 he required his apprentice clerks to learn Pitman's system. There were later rivals and successors *eg* John Robert Gregg who published his system in 1888, but it was Pitman's which was adopted by the commercial schools when they opened, thereby ensuring its pride of place.

Shorthand, however, is only as good as the person using it. An article in the American journal *The Business Man's Magazine* of 1905 asked with some frustration though no little humour 'Will someone please explain how we may account for the obtuseness of the average stenographer ... I speak of her whom the "business colleges" are letting loose in ever-increasing multitudes?' He quotes many examples of mis-transcribed shorthand, 'a stream of eloquence' becoming 'a string of elephants' on one occasion. Of one (dismissed) stenographer he mused: 'how she ever managed to operate her "Remington" through such an entanglement of

Right
Two extracts from the manuscript of Samuel Pepys's Diary. Far from being in code, the Diary uses a system of shorthand devised by Thomas Shelton, who published his first manual of instruction in 1626. Note that many proper names are written 'in clear'. Perhaps the myth of the Diary being written in code arose from the omission of the 'naughty bits' (which Pepys disguises but thinly) when the Diary was first published.

January

[Year 1660-1., Vol.1.]

5 〜 ⌁ 〉 ⋁⁻3 ∴ ℰ ρ ρ 2 ⟨ ⊢ 113 ∧ ⌁ ⟩ 4

Tom: Fuller ⌐. φ 2 ⟨ 2 ⁓ ∧ ⌒3 ℰ∧

⋁ ⌐ 〈 ⌐. ⋏ ∧ ⁓ 2 4. 2 Jamaica o℄

2 ℏ⁻ ⟨⋌ 43 θ. ℬ′ 2⟩ ∴

3 2 Dr. hall 2 ⟨ ⁝ 〜. ⁊ ♂ ⁔⁻ —

⋁ o ⌐⁻ — ⅌ o ⌐⁻ ⋁3 ⁓ ⟨ α ⁔ —

o⁺ ⌁⁻ 2 Dr. ⁓ hall 3 2 Wills ⁔²

o Spiver — o⁺ ⁻ Cash 〜 ⁝3 ∧ ⁓ 9

Pauls ℂ ⟨⁻ 2 ⁝ 〉⁻ Ogilby's Æsop's fables

— Tullys officys 2 b ⟨⁊ ℇ ⟨ ∴ ℐ 〜 —

2 〉⁻ ∴

February

[Year 1661-2., Vol.II.]

Musiq ⁊⁻ ∧ ∞ ⊘ ∴ — 2 Pauls ℂ ⟨⁻ — ⁓ ⌐ o D⁻

Fullers Englands worthys ∴ ⟨ ⋁⁊ ⟩ ⟩ . ♂ ρ ⁓ — S. ρ⁻

2 ⋁3 q ⁓ ⁓ ⁓ ⊥ 2 ⋏ τ⁻ 〉⁺ . ⊨ ℇ ⟨ ⟩ 43 ∴ —

S. ⋁ρ — ∇ 〜 2 ⁔⁻ 3 ⟩ ⍵ ⟨ (⊨ o h ℒ 2⊬ o ⟍

⁺ ⟍ ⁺⁺ — armiy) o ℓℓ ⁊⁊ ♂ ⁓ — ⁔⁻ ⁺ 6 o⁻ q Cambr

⁻ Norfolk ∴ ⟨ . 6 ♂⁻ g ⁺⁺ ⁻ ⁻⁊⁻ ⌐⁊⁻⌐

♂ 〜 ⁓ ⟨ α ⁔ — — ♂ ⁔ 2 〉⁻ ∴

PHONOGRAPHY, OR WRITING by SOUND, being also A New & Natural SYSTEM OF SHORT HAND.

Engraved & Printed by S.J. Lawes, High St. Bristol.

13. When two vowels begin or end a word put one close & the other at a little distance as iota, oasis. Isaiah, Victoria.

14. Never join a short straight letter (which is always a double or treble cons.) to a letter in the same direction, but write the single cons. for it, or take off the pen, as "fault" or "not" "steam ed" or "not" "started"

15. Shn after n & r, and before r is curved thus as nation, portion, missionary.

16. Make the stroke s in these cases only, when a word contains only s & a vowel, as ves) sigh) when s is repeated as cease) assizes) also when a word begins with a vowel followed by s, as ask) or ends with a vowel preceded by s, as tendency) & whenever you want to put a vowel to s, as sumptuous or

17. All rules relating to the sharp consonants p, t, ch, k, f, th, s, sh, are also applicable to their correspond flats. b, d, j, g, v, th, z, zh.

18. When sh or l stands alone, count the vowels places downwards, as shoe law callow. When either letter is joined to the loop s only, write it downwards, as issues lace sale

19. Make r and shn with a tick when either letter stands alone, as or rye ocean & when it is succeeded by the loop s only, as arise airs oceans

20. The letters chn & rch must never stand alone, nor with the loop s only added, because of sht & rl.

21. Each letter in the Alphabet stands for the words put to it. (except the examples in short hand) & all others of the same sound, as I and eye, &c for other words write all the consonants that sound (joining them together,) & the principal vowels, as appeared

22. S may be added to an Alphabetical word without taking off the pen, as words thoughts hands thinks Other letters must be separated, as established distinction

23. The horizontal & half sized cons. (k.m, nd &c.) when representing words, stand at the top of the line for words contain. first place vowels, and at the bottom for words cont. second & third place vowels. In the Alphabet, these words are divided by a colon.

24. All middle place vowels (o.wa, &c) when standing alone, go at the bottom of the line, as away yet one

25. Compound words must be reduced to their primitives, and written near together, as within without altogether somewhat yourselves

26. Disjoin Prefixes & Affixes, as interest? Phonography or for a plural-affix add s, as subscriptions) tenements earldoms

27. Coin & con are written by a light dot before the next cons. as comply consider & accom by a heavy dot as accommodate accomplished

28. For ing put a small dot after the last cons. as starting [the plural is a large dot, as workings

29. If a word reaches too low, or does not join well, take off the pen, as constituted chargeable

30. Choose the best manner of writing a word, as part not armor not

31. Generally omit h, for the sake of brevity, as comprehensive

32. A first place vowel, standing at the beginning of a word, should be written in point of time, before the cons. to which it is placed as peaceable

33. FIGURES. Write the digits thus. 0, 1, 2, 3, 4, 5, 6, 7, 8, 9. Put all other numbers in short-hand words, as 20 46 or join the digits, placing a line under as 396 666 1840 6862

34. STOPS. Comma Semicolon Colon Period or leave 1/4 1/2 1 inch spaces. Hyphen. Irony Exclamation(!) & all other stops & marks as usual. Italic. See Psalm 133. Accent. décent noble deny tarry present present Inflection: rise fall as is it so or so?

35. Reader, Practise & Persevere

exist only in provincialisms & Foreign Languages, are not noticed here, they will be in the Large Plate, six times the size of this, to be published May 1st 1840. Price 8s also in 8 c.8

JOINING TABLE

B T J K V TH S Z H L R M N H B H D T K G F V Sh M N A N N V C K
(table of shorthand joining symbols — P, CH, C, G, L, R, M, N, B, T, J, K, L, R rows)

The dots shew where to begin the 22 SINGLE & 96 DOUBLE CONSONANTS, but form no part of them,

P.	up, upon.
.pt	wrapped
P.l	principle,
P.r	partic, portion.
B.	be-en, but.
	before, bility.
.bd	robbed
B.l	public breadth.
B.r	re-member.
T.	out, time,
t.l	till, little.
T.r	truth, trans.
t.n	ten, town.
D.	day, done.
d.l	deliver-y
D.r	dear, D.
d.n	down, London.
CH.	which,
.cht	fetched
ch.l	children
ch.r	natur-
ch.n	question
J.	Jesus, general
.jd	obliged
j.l	individual,
j.r	Jerusalem
j.n	margin

K.	king: com.
.kt	object: perfect
K.l	call, calculation
K.r	CHRIST: carry
.kn	cannot: can.
G.	give-n: gave.
	go, together
.gd	GOD: good.
G.l	glor-y, glad.
G.r	great, graph
.gn	begin-ning.
	again-st
	for, if, off, for
F.	
.ft	after, left
F.l	full, follow.
F.r	from, fre-often
fn	often, (quent.)
V.	have, ever.
.vd	loved
V.l	evil, volume.
V.r	every, advan
	even, heaven.
.vn	thought, hath.
TH	
th.l	Bethel
TH.r	through,
TH.l	that, the
th.r	for, withered
th.n	their, whether

S.	saw, society, so
o	object us, salt, &c, circum (for general use)
	call (for partic.)
	system, scription
Z.	h-is h-as, whose.
	it is, Israel
	shal, ship.
SH	
.shl	washed
sh.l	e-special (shire
SH.r	as-sure, share.
shn	auction
ZH	
zhl	azure
	usual,
zhl	treasury
	occasion
L.	LORD, also
.lp	help, (ly, ally.
.lb	elbow
.lt	difficult-y.
.ld	hold, world.
	filch, fold
.lj	indulge
.lk	milk
	wolf
.lf	alphabet-ical
.lv	resolve
.lth	health.

.lth	although
.lsh	Welsh
.lzh	color
.lr	already.
.lm	ALMIGHTY
.ln	fallen
R (See Rule 19)	are, or.
	our, recom
.rp	sharps
.rb	suburbs
.rt	heart, short
.rd	word, heard
.rch	church, accord
.rj	charges
.rk	work, borg
.rg	burg, Sweden

.rf	scarf
.rv	preserve
.rth	earth, forth
.rth	worthy
.rsh	marsh
.rzh	curled
.rl	real, rule
.rm	form, concern
.rn	morning
M	mere: more
	mine: me: may
	am, multi, ment
.mp	important
.mt	meet, might
.md	a-mid-st mod-e
.ml	mercy.
M.	mere: more

.N	on, any, no.
	own in com: uncom
.nt	want into: went
.nd	hand, under
.nch	French, ind
.nj	change, journal
.nl	nor, honor-able
NG	thing, Engl
	language
.ngk	distinct.
	think, thank
.ngg	single, ang
H.	he, him, had
.hr	here. hood

SUMMARY of the SINGLE CONS. 8 Mutes 8 Semivowels, 2 Liquids, 3 Nasals, 1 Aspirate. Pronounce each of the 65 TREBLE CONSONANTS at once as p·rd dpt sorted vrvd &c and rd (the past tense) is added to a hooked letter by making it half length, as tld rtitled rvd deserved. These Treble Cons. represent the past tenses of the verbs placed to the Double Cons. from which they are derived as carried. Note: spr represents spirit-ual, str strong, strength; skr scriptur-al.

THE LORD's INVITATION. Matthew 11. 28 to 30. Written in full.

29 ...
... 30 ...

Any Language may be written in Phonog. with a trifling difference in the sound of some letters. French German

Isaac Pitman's shorthand system.

Above
The coveted certificate of proficiency.

Left
'Any person may receive lessons from the Author by post gratuitously. Each lesson must be enclosed in a paid letter. The pupil can write about a dozen verses from the Bible, leaving spaces between the lines for the corrections.'

lace, ribbons, ties, bracelets and chains has ever remained a gloomy and unsolved mystery'. Her 'all-pervading odour of cheap perfumery' might have been endured had her 'copy' been good. He concludes, however, that despite the transcriptions making absolutely no sense, for $12 – 15 a week the presence of female stenographers 'somehow lightens the daily grind'.

Shorthand in the office went a long way to meet the mid-century need for greater speed and accuracy. But to whom could the next set of letters be dictated if the clerk was away transcribing the last set? Clearly there was a need for some means of recording a dictated letter and saving it for transcription when time was available.

The dictating machine

Recording and reproducing the human voice had been a challenge since the late 18th century. In April 1877 Charles Cros, a French amateur scientist, wrote a paper describing a method by which the human voice could cause vibrations in a membrane; producing a tracing on lamp-blacked glass which was photo-engraved on a metal disc. Another membrane moving over the photo-engraved trace reproduced the original sounds. Cros could find no one sufficiently interested to invest in his discovery, so he donated his idea to the *Académie des Sciences* in Paris.

In August of the same year, Thomas Edison sketched a metallic cylinder around which a helical groove had been cut, mounted on a shaft with a screw of the same pitch. On top of the cylinder was a diaphragm with a stylus sticking out which could be moved into the groove.

The sketch was translated into a reality. The cylinder was covered in tinfoil. Edison spoke into a horn, activating the diaphragm whose needle was in contact with the foil. In spite of the historical importance of the occasion, Edison was seized with the paralysis ever after known to those faced with a recorder for the first time and could think of nothing to say but 'Mary had a little lamb ... ' He wound the cylinder back to its starting position, positioned the needle on the groove and lo! there was Mary again.

The potential for such an instrument was grasped immediately. Edison was working for Western Union at the time and his over-riding thoughts were with the

Edison's historic sketch of 12 August 1877, asking his assistant John Kruesi to build the apparatus depicted - the tinfoil phonograph.

implications of his invention for office work. However, the entertainment possibilities did not escape him and it was of course the entertainments industry which embraced the phonograph – and gramophone – and made them its own.

The office was not neglected, however, as the technology was interchangeable and in the 1880s the audio-stenographer was born. One of Edison's later ideas was for a 'telescribe' – a means of coupling the phonograph to the telephone to record messages.

The typewriter

But it was the typewriter which gave the office revolution the next turn. When Queen Victoria came to the throne in 1837 the typewriter was virtually unknown.

By the end of her reign in 1901 few of even the staidest offices were without one.

The idea of a writing machine was not new. A patent granted to Henry Mill in 1714 sounds interesting, but the passage of time has obliterated any useful record of how his machine worked. In 1711 James Rawson made a machine which 'amazed all beholders'. This had small keys like a keyboard instrument. Long steel rods carrying brass squares engraved with letters were attached to a steel frame. When the keys were pressed down the rods struck an inked ribbon. The movement was driven by a powerful spring.

Two strands keep weaving through the development of typewriters: one was the likeness in action in many developers' minds to the keyboards of musical instruments: the other was the kinship between a mechanical writer and a machine for embossing letters for the blind.

William Austin Burt (1729–1858) showed an ingenious backwoodsman's approach with his 'Typographer'. It certainly worked, and we have his letter to prove it, but was never manufactured. Such was the abundance of ideas being registered in the patent offices of Europe and America that *Scientific American* was confident enough to predict (6 July 1867) that 'the laborious and unsatisfactory performance of the pen must sooner or later become obsolete for general purposes'. The unsung heroes dallied with keys arranged as on an instrument, in a circle; some used pedals, others levers: the paper might feed in flat or wind around a cylinder. One of the difficulties with a cylindrical platen is that the type has to correspond with the platen's curve otherwise the impression is uneven. Many ideas were excellent and in advance of those incorporated in the model that in the end 'made it' and their exponents are examples of men beavering away without any commercial interest or backing – clear cases of 'not what you know but whom you know'. For example, Peter Hood, a Scot, produced a machine which fulfilled four essential ingredients: the type was brought to a common printing point; the paper moved step by step, the type was inked, and the writing visible, but we hear no more of it.

The machine eventually produced commercially was the result of the labour of Christopher Latham Sholes (1819–90) of Milwaukee, Wisconsin. He was a printer and publisher by trade, as well as a newspaper

Thomas Edison with an early phonograph. Turning the handle screws the drum along beneath the stylus mounted on the fixed diaphragm. The flywheel on the left does its best to keep the speed reasonably constant.

editor and minor public official. His patent was granted in 1868 and he was the first to coin the word 'typewriter'.

Because of the circles in which he moved, Sholes knew many people with a professional interest in 'typewriters' and was able to send his prototype and subsequent 'improvements' to these interested parties for their comments. One of the test lines for the machines was the then current political slogan encouraging the Republicans to forget their internal squabbles: 'Now is the time for all good men to come to the aid of their party.' The teething troubles of developing the typewriter were enormous and a continuous supply of funds was needed. The main backer – and indeed the inspiration preventing Sholes from giving up – was James Densmore of Meadville, Pennsylvania, a lawyer

The Discavox recording machine (1936).

NEW PRODUCT REPORT

DICTAPHONE DICTATING MACHINE
Cameo Model

[Reference should be made to the Cross Index
which heads this Section (2.31)]

Introduced: November, 1939.

Dictaphone Corporation (See Dictaphone Recording Apparatus
June, 1937.)

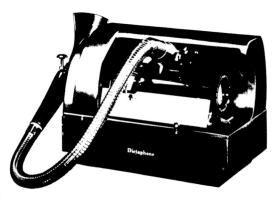

The Dictaphone dictating machine (1939).

General

The new Cameo Model is the latest addition to the Dictaphone line of dictating equipment. The width, height and weight are less than any previous model, and while this reduction in size tends to increase its utility as a desk or portable model, it can also be used satisfactorily with either the DeLuxe or Progress cabinets.

Two special carrying cases are available, with space for four cylinders.

From *The London Phonographer* 1891.

Below

Charles Thurber's typewriter of 1845. The circular 'gallery' carries three groups of character keys. Each key has a mother-of-pearl button, and a character engraved on its lower end. The desired character is brought into position by turning the gallery, and its key depressed to ink it and print it on the paper. The travelling and revolving platen to carry the paper is an essential element of the invention.

Right.
Facsimile letter produced on 'Thurber's Mechanical Chirographer'.

NORWICH 3. FEBRUARY 1845.

GENT.

WE HAVE, AT LENGTH COMPLETED ONE OF THURBERS MECHANICAL CHIROGRAPHERS. ALTHOUGH YOU WILL NOTICE IMPERFECTIONS IN THE FORMATION OF THE LETTERS IN THIS COMMUNICATION, YET THERE IS NOT A SINGLE DEFECT WHICH DOES NOT ADMIT OF AN EASY AND PERFECT REMEDY. I AM PERFECTLY SATISFIED WITH IT BECAUSE I DID NOT LOOK FOR PERFECTION IN THIS FIRST MACHINE. THE DIFFICULTY IN THIS MACHINE IS THAT THE CAMS ARE NOT LARGE ENOUGH. THIS, OF COURSE, CAN BE AVOIDED. I THINK MR. KELLAR TOLD WHEN I LAST SAW HIM THAT IF I WOULD WRITE TO HIM INFORMING HIM WHEN I SHOULD BE IN WASHINGTON HE MIGHT BE ABLE TO MAKE SOME SUGGESTIONS ABOUT A HOME DURING MY STAY IN WASHINGTON. I SHALL WISH TO EXHIBIT THE MACHINE. TO SUCH GENTLEMEN AS MIGHT TAKE INTEREST IN A THING OF THIS KIND. I DO NOT WISH TO MAKE A PUBLIC SHOW OF MYSELF OR MY MACHINE. I WANT TO SHOW IT TO MEN WHO CAN APPRECIATE AND UNDERSTAND MACHINERY. MR. ROCKWELL. OUR REPRESENTATIVE IN CONGRESS VOLUNTEERED TO GET ME A ROOM & I HAVE WRITTEN TO HIM ON THE SUBJECT. STILL I THOUGHT IN CONSEQUENCE OF YOUR MORE THOROUGH ACQUAINTANCE IN THE CITY THAT YOU MIGHT BE ABLE TO MAKE SOME SUGGESTIONS WHICH MIGHT BE BENEFICIAL TO ME IN EXHIBITING HE MACHINE. I WANT A ROOM LARGE ENOUGH TO RECEIVE SUCH COMPANY AS MAY WISH TO SEE THE MACHINE. I WANT A ROOM WHERE I CAN SAFELY LEAVE IT WHEN I AM ABSENT AND WHERE NO ONE WOULD BE LIABLE TO GO IN AND INJURE IT. EXCUSE THE LIBERTY I HAVE TAKEN, AND BELIEVE ME

YOURS, TRULY.   CHARLES THURBER.

MESSRS. KELLER & GREENOUGH
PATENT ATTORNIES.
WASHINGTON. D. C.

and small-scale inventor himself.

Scholes was essentially a tinkerer rather than an inventor, but one of those with a likely interest whose curiosity was briefly engaged was Thomas Edison. He fiddled around and produced what he called 'fair results' but in the 1870s his concentration was elsewhere, though he did think he 'might invent an electric typewriter – a noiseless one', one day.

By 1872 Sholes was financially ruined and had to sell his interest. This eventually passed to the Remington family business which included guns, sewing machines and farm machinery. It did mean, however incongruous, that finance and technical expertise were available to enable many teasing problems to be solved. Remington's typewriters were sold in Great Britain in 1874, though the real impact was made upon the world after 1882 when a separate Remington typewriter company was established as an international selling agency. In 1879 146 machines were sold; by 1890 sales had reached 65,000 a year. In 1887 the American correspondent of the *Phonetic Journal* reported to its British readership that 'typewriting has become quite fashionable even among the upper classes here'.

Ladies were trained in typewriting and 'sold' along with the machine so it should not become an expensive luxury. As early as 1881 the Young Women's Christian Association in America foresaw the possibilities of typing as a female career and started a class for eight girls. Five years later it was estimated some 60,000 girls were tapping away in the United States.

Because of their arrangement, the typebars on the Sholes machine had a tendency to collide and stick to one another. Working on the principle that no one would ever want to use more than two fingers for typing, Sholes decided to arrange the letters so that the most often used were the furthest apart. This was fine for a while.

Then Mrs LB Longley, the owner of a shorthand and typewriting school in Cincinnati, had the audacity to suggest that typists should use all ten of their fingers. A 'duel' was fought between a four-finger champion Mr Louis Taub and a ten-finger champion Mr McGurrin. After 45 minutes of copy typing and 45 minutes dictation on to the typewriter Mr McGurrin was the clear winner: during the copy-typing his eyes never left the copy. 'Hunt and peck' gave way indisputably to 'touch typing'.

A typewriter of 1836. The rotating arm selects the character; depressing the knob positions and prints it.

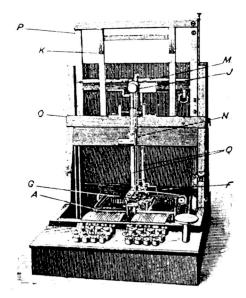

Pratt's experimental typewriter.

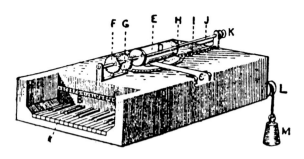

An early Sholes machine with piano-type keyboard. The weight M provides power to wind the ribbon and move the paper for letter and line spacing.

A Blickensderfer, or 'Blick', machine about 1893. Depressing a key causes the type drum to turn and bob to bring the desired character into position before it wipes across the ink pad and strikes an impression on the paper.

A skeletonic Sholes prototype about 1870.

Teachers of typing thereafter became the greatest force in preventing Sholes' 'standard' letter arrangement being changed to the 'ideal' proposed by JB Hammond – even though Hammond's layout was arguably swifter to operate.

Machines, then, were definitely on the office scene by the turn of the century. Franz Wagner is credited with the first 'visible' machine in 1894. It was a 'front stroke' machine, previous models having been 'understroke' ones with the type not visible. Mr Odin wrote in *Typewriter Topics*: 'The typewriter has released the business man from all limitation and restriction.' Sir Arthur Conan Doyle even had Sherlock Holmes solving *A Case of Identity* by correctly identifying the impostor's typewriter.

Phonetic Journal of 2 November 1901 reported on 'the possibility of removing the shorthand-typist from the business office to some central exchange where he or she can take notes of letters dictated by telephone, transcribe the letters on the typewriter, and afterwards deliver them to their respective business houses from which they had been dictated over the telephone'. This was a plea for the 'typing pool' which was already being used by the National Telephone Company in London. An important consideration was that 'the noise of the typewriter is removed from the office so that it doesn't interfere with ordinary work'. This also removed 'any objection which may be held to the employment of female typists.'

When war broke out in 1914 typewriter production in Europe ground to a halt. American production continued, and the 30 or more manufacturers were able to meet the renewed demand, at whatever price, in the 1920s. Development then forged ahead and the main interest was in electrifying the machines.

The electric typewriter

Edison had taken out a patent for an electric typewriter in 1871 with G Arrington. He had realised that manual ones were difficult to manage for ladies in a 'cage of whalebone and steel' and lamented the amount of

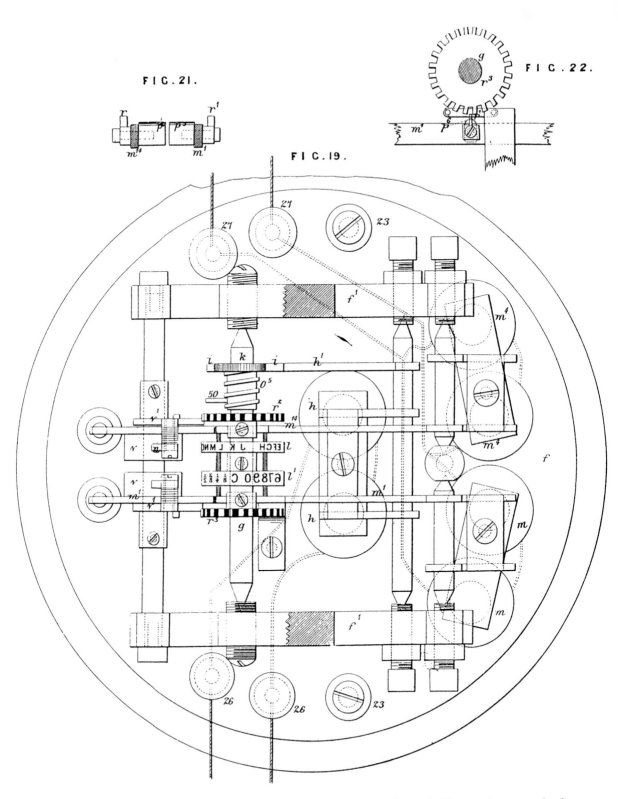

FIG.21.

FIG.22.

FIG.19.

A drawing from Edison's British patent no 1,453 of 1872 for a printing telegraph. The rotating typewheels are clearly seen, as are the plan views of several actuating electromagnets.

The Hammond typewriter in about 1895. Interchangeable type sectors are carried on the ring between the ribbon spools. An even impression is obtained by striking the paper from the back, pressing it on to the ribbon against the selected character. Like many early machines, the Hammond has a certain bare elegance.

cleaning and oiling typists had to carry out. Not for a while though were all functions electrified, one of the last being the carriage return. In a 1925 New York Exhibition of Office Machinery Remington showed its first all-electric model. It even had a 'slave' model which repeated the action of the master machine simultaneously. This went on sale in 1927 but its unreliability delayed public acceptance. The touch was quite different and early machines gave an enormous jolt when the carriage returned.

Office Equipment Magazine of April 1923 reviewed a few of the 'numerous varieties' of the typewriter that then existed. The electric model, the 'Mercedes Electra' excited little comment beyond the observation that the impression was uniform, not depending upon strength of the strike. The Noiseless Typewriter however was commented upon very favourably. Although 'noiseless' machines had been in existence for some time, their name represented a slight exaggeration.

Now, however, the machines have been modified 'to suit the business man who suffers from nerves'. The reviewer was awaiting the deluge of salesmen from America where these machines were seemingly ubiquitous.

Apart from 'nerves' another health hazard in the 1920s office was apparently 'typewriter glare'. 'I am informed' said the reviewer in *Office Equipment* 'that the glare of the keys has for some time been a matter which has excited considerable interest amongst the medical profession, it being suggested that this has been one of the causes of nervous breakdowns'. Perhaps today's European directives on office practice are driven by similar fears.

It was not really till after the Second World War (during which production again subsided), that electric typewriters were satisfactorily refined, by which time acceptance of such machines was much more widespread. In Great Britain in 1952, 450 electric machines were sold. By 1972 the annual figure was 80,000.

Seeking an alternative power to electricity, Marshal A Weir produced (1891) a pneumatic machine which indeed reduced the manual effort and the noise while increasing the speed. The main drawback was the slow return of the typebars.

IBM's first electric typewriter was sold in the 1930s. In the late 1950s the company produced the 'Executive' which had proportional spacing – that is to say that, as in typesetting, i and j occupied less width than M and W. The machine also had two space bars giving a choice of two-unit and three-unit spaces. One of its advantages was that it could produce 'justified' copy – that is, with a straight right-hand margin. You typed the copy once, measured the number of units it was short of a full line, and typed it again with extra spaces inserted accordingly. The process was tedious, and demanded complete accuracy. In 1960, Rodney Dale built a prototype attachment for an IBM Executive which enabled it to justify semi-automatically, but the device was rejected by IBM. A possible reason for this emerged the following year when IBM brought out the Selectric or 'golf-ball' model.

The 'golf-ball' mechanism was a sphere mounted on a carrier which bobbed around and along. The models took up less space because there was no moving carriage. They produced less vibration than a conventional machine, and the golf ball could be interchanged with others presenting different type faces. The golf-ball action was reminiscent of that of the Blickensderfer of 1893, or the one-hand, two-fingers Mignon of 1903 and, later, the Teletype. Later came the IBM 72 composer, which incorporated automatic justification and started the next revolution in rudimentary mechanical desktop publishing.

Desktop publishing

As computers became smaller and more powerful, some of the technology spilled into typewriters. The electric typewriter became electronic, with a built-in memory, and sometimes with a limited display of what had been typed, and sometimes with a spell-checking facility.

But these machines were fighting a losing battle against the desktop computer which could do so much more than a 'mere typewriter'. Suites of software (programs) were developed embracing word processing, calculating 'spreadsheets', and facilities for preparing and inserting tables and graphics. A range of typefaces was developed, and for a time desktop publishing (DTP) encouraged amateurs to produce material completely lacking in design taste. Fortunately, it seems that the worst excesses of bad DTP are behind us, and many users now realize that there is an art called 'typography' to be approached with respect. Once dismissive of the new medium, 'proper' typographers soon espoused its capabilities and the equipment has now become not only acceptable to traditional designers and printers (than whom few are more traditional) but also adopted more and more widely for its capacity to perform in completely new ways – indeed this book was set using DTP.

The office has taken much of this capability in its stride, and the appearance and layout of letters and documents has undergone the greatest change since the passing of the scribe and scrivener.

Right
The pneumatically-operated automatic typewriter produces standard sales letters, stopping only for the operator to 'personalize' them, and load more paper. One operator could sit on a swivel chair and attend to four machines one after the other – hence the reference to '4 machines as a window display'.

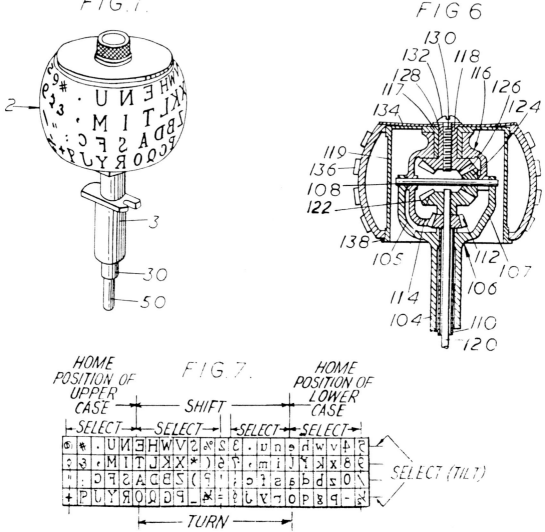

Type head of the IBM 'golf-ball' typewriter from British patent no 842,328 of 1960. The first American application was filed in 1955. The interchangeable type heads provide one machine with a range of faces. Depressing a key causes the head to turn and tilt to bring the desired character into position. Moving the type head and its ribbon cassette along the platen (roller) instead of moving a heavy carriage past the type head made for a compact, fast, quiet and vibration-free machine. The type head principle is similar to that of the Blickensderfer (see page 23), but the arrangement of concentric shafts and gears within the head is far more elegant.

THE "VIROTYP" — A POCKET TYPEWRITER

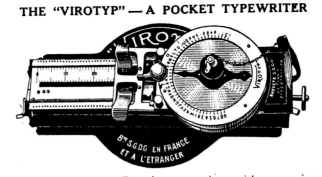

The "Virotyp" pocket typewriter is a French invention. It is of the size and thickness of a pocketbook, and can be used no matter whether you are in a tramway, motor omnibus or motor car. The shaking of a train in motion or any other mode of traveling does not allow use of a pencil or fountain pen in the production of writing easily read, but the "Virotyp" typewriter does. The machine is more easily put into your pocket than a big newspaper or magazine.

The weight is only 450 grammes, and the width is 9 centimetres, by 15½ centimetres long. The thickness is 38 millimetres. The makers claim that it is not a toy, but a really serviceable writing machine. Not much instruction is needed to initiate anyone into its use, and almost anybody can write with it immediately. The alignment is good, and three carbon copies can be obtained. The keyboard includes the necessary signs and characters for letter writing, and the machine is guaranteed for one year by the manufacturers. The "Virotyp" is the outcome of long study to produce a real pocket typewriter with a carriage. The inventor is French and the machine is of entirely French manufacture. The "Virotyp" machine, if placed on its support, can be used for correspondence like a big typewriter, and commercial letters, envelopes, bills and so on can be done with it. The machine is patented in England, Germany and America.

The manufacturers are open to sell the patents for the United States and Great Britain and Colonies. Should they not come to satisfactory arrangements to sell patents in those countries, they would appoint agents. For all other countries the world over they solicit enquiries for agencies. Write for further particulars to The Virotyp Typewriter, 12, rue du Hanovre, Paris, France, from which place inquiries will be promptly handled.

If the claims of the manufacturers hold true, it seems that this handy little device will fill a long felt want among traveling men who are tired of the old-fashioned pen, and who desire a serviceable machine to take care of their correspondence.

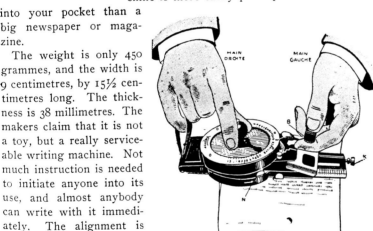

Information acquires a technology

In societies where people have property rights, the importance of accurate records is paramount. There is no need to record if there are no questions as to who owns what. But when people have rights, questions will arise about the transferral, the boundaries, the worth and not least the management of those rights.

Recording information

The need to record political speeches accurately has been recognized since ancient times, but the development of a clerical industry devoted to the recording and management of transactions is a result of the increased acquisition of – and trade in – property by the church, kings and barons in medieval times.

For taxation purposes it was necessary to know who owned what and it is a measure of the sophistication of the society that it was taken for granted that both parties had to agree to that ownership. 'Memory' and 'custom' were still greatly respected but by the end of the 13th century the keeping of estate accounts formed part of the curriculum at Oxford University and as Alan Delgado says in *The Enormous File*, it was a 'surprisingly early origin for university business studies'.

Tally sticks bore notches of different sizes indicating, for example, financial amounts. The notches were

The Chinese abacus or *swanpan*, similar to the Roman abacus, works with a combination of binary and one-to-one representations.

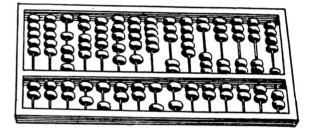

Tally sticks: assignment to Frederick Mynhard Franklin of five Exchequer annuities with wood tallies dated 1698-1705.

John Napier of Merchiston, Edinburgh (1550-1617), 'the famous inventor of the Logarithms, the Person to whom the title of Great Man is more justly due than to any other, whom his country ever produced.'

made symmetrically along both sides of the stick's length, and the stick then split in two. Each party to the transaction then kept one half of the stick which therefore always 'tallied' with the other half. This basic form of contract was not legally abolished until the end of the 18th century, though its use continued into the 19th century.

Financiers, bankers, merchants and kept their accounts on parchment in what amounted to some early double-entry book-keeping: financial transactions were written on one side and matched produce or whatever on the other. The origin of double-entry book-keeping can be traced to Italy early in the 14th century.

Computation

Commerce and trade increased in Britain and other Western European nations rapidly from the 16th century onwards and, while clerks needed above all to be accurate arithmeticians, various aids were employed to help compute large sums. The abacus, for example, had been in use since ancient times, but from the 17th century Napier's 'rods', or 'bones', were used.

Napier's rods were enormously popular. But Napier was only one of a number of great mathematicians in the 17th century who, among other things, strove to devise a mechanical means of computation. One of the problems was to devise a means of 'carrying' from one column of figures to the next. This was solved by the German William Schickard in 1623, but details of his machine were lost soon after, so many have credited the French scientist and philosopher Blaise Pascal (1623–62) with the invention of the mechanical calculator. His 'Pascaline' (circa 1642) worked well for addition but was otherwise mechanically unreliable.

Neither the Pascaline, nor (understandably) the slide rule invented by Edmund Gunter and Revd William Oughtred, was much used by clerks and bookkeepers. However, these devices, along with Leibnitz's stepped reckoner of the 1690s, are milestones on the path leading to the tabulator of the 19th century and the calculator of the 20th.

It must be said, however, that these lofty thinkers were not out to produce a simple office aid. The job of mathematicians in the 17th, 18th and 19th centuries was to calculate tables for engineers, navigators, scientists and ballistics experts. The efforts in the 19th

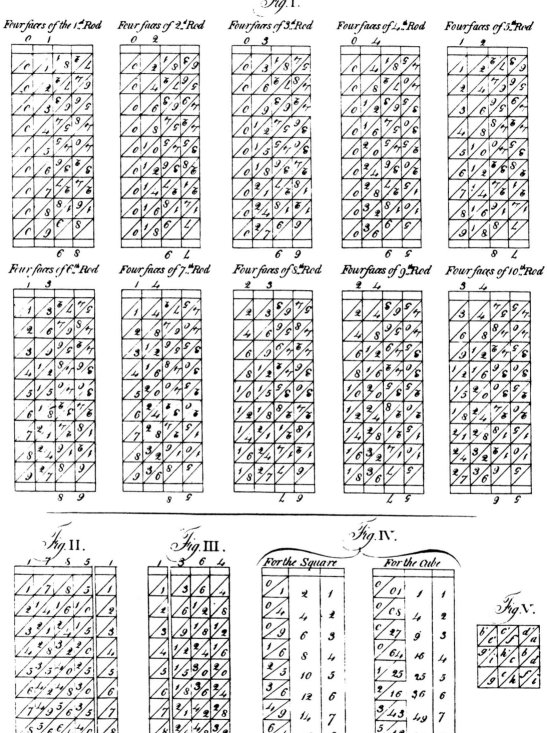

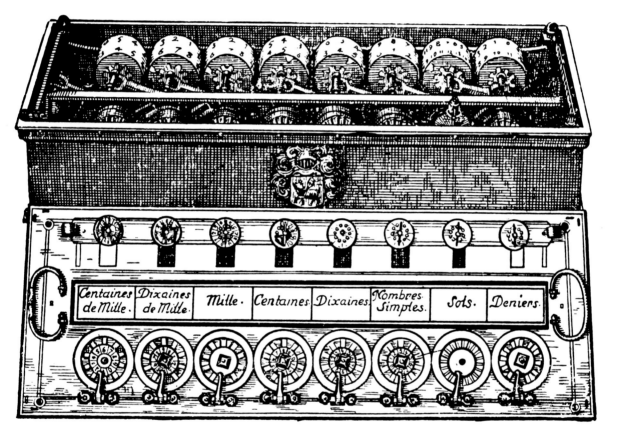

A slide rule, showing the logarithmic scales, fixed and sliding, and the sliding 'cursor'. The slide rule works on the principle that numbers may be multiplied and divided by adding and subtracting their logarithms.

Above

The Pascaline with top cover removed. The digits are designated from 100,000 on the left to 0.01 on the right. The cunning lies in its ability to 'carry'; each complete revolution of a wheel, or drum, steps its higher neighbour on by one digit.

Left

A set of John Napier's rods (or bones). Each block represents the four faces of a square rod. To prepare, say, the 365 times table, the faces of the rods for 3, 6 and 5 are laid side by side. If we wish to multiply by seven, we look at the seventh row of the rods, which will read 2/1 4/2 3/5. Now we add the figures between the oblique strokes to get the answer: 365 x 7 = 2,555.

Leibnitz's calculating machine. As with the Pascaline, its secret lies in its ability to carry as numbers are added.

AN ARITHMOMETER WITH TEN FIGURES.

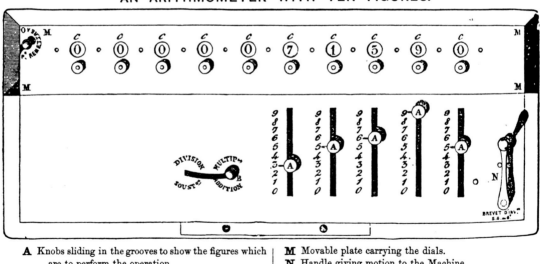

A Knobs sliding in the grooves to show the figures which are to perform the operation.
B White knob showing the rule to be performed.
C Opening exhibiting the results.

M Movable plate carrying the dials.
N Handle giving motion to the Machine.
O Knob serving to replace the figures of the plate **M** at **O**.

The panel of Thomas de Colmar's Arithmometer. 'Anyone the least acquainted with ciphering will be able to perform all the Arithmetical rules, and the learned will solve with facility the most intricate problems, being at the same time relieved from the trouble of making calculations requiring a vast deal of time and labour.' It was said that two eight-figure numbers could be multiplied in 18 seconds.

century to mechanize some of the drudgery in these calculations led to the technology behind the office 'spin-offs'.

Charles Xavier Thomas de Colmar in France invented his Arithmometer in 1820. An insurance agent, it is indicative of the amount of business he was handling that he felt it worth while to invest his energies in a device to ease his job. The Arithmometer was based upon Leibnitz's stepped reckoner and was the first multiplication machine to be produced commercially for general sale.

Charles Babbage

The Englishman Charles Babbage (1792–1871), gentleman and scientist, was excessively pedantic, and irritated by the errors in the arithmetical and logarithmic tables of his time. Such tables were compiled by an army of calculating clerks and, seeing that such work could be mechanized, Babbage conceived a machine which would produce tables without error. In 1821, he announced his intention of building a 'difference engine' to members of the Royal Astronomical Society.

The following year, he won the Society's first gold medal with his 'Observations on the application of machinery to the computation of mathematical tables', supported by a pilot model of his machine.

Following this acclaim, Babbage began work on his full-scale difference engine, designed not only to calculate mathematical tables, but also to print them. He started with a government grant of £1,500, but the work went on and on, consuming £6,000 of Babbage's own money, and £17,000 from the government, before a halt was called. Only incomplete parts of the unfinished engine now remain.

Undeterred, Babbage began to design an even more ambitious project – a general-purpose computer designed to perform a range of sophisticated functions. Babbage's analytical engine was years ahead of its time; it embodied the idea of stored programming, working on a punched card system (similar to the one Joseph Marie Jacquard had designed for his patterning loom). Work started in 1834, and by 1840 Babbage had published his twenty-fifth design. He spent the rest of his life on and off in a search for perfection, but the

---

Why 'difference engine'?

Suppose we want to find the values of $x = n^3 + 2n^2 + 3n + 4$, for a series of values of n.

First, assign a sequence of values to n:

n	1	2	3	4	5	6

Then work out x $(=n^3+2n^2+3n+4)$.

x	10	26	58	112	194	310

Now subtract each value of x from the next: (26–10), (58–26), (112–58) and so on.

S_1	16	32	54	82	116

And continue the process: (32–16), (54–32), (82–54) and so on.

S_2	16	22	28	34

Until each subtraction gives the same result:

S_3	6	6	6

Now we can turn the process the other way up.

If we start with the row of sixes and keep adding to the starting figure of each row (16, 16, 10) we will be able to calculate the table of values of x without any more pain than adding differences:

S_3			6	6	6	6	6	6	6	. . . . .
S_2		16	22	28	34	40	46	52	58	. . . . .
S_1	16	32	54	82	116	156	202	254	312	. . . . .
x	10	26	58	112	194	310	466	668	922	1234 . . . . .
n	1	2	3	4	5	6	7	8	9	10 . . . .

This will work for any equation.

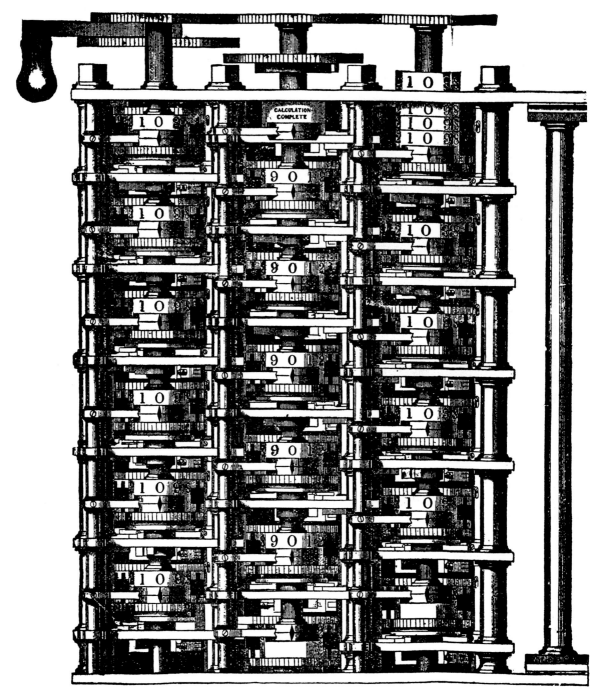

CALCULATION COMPLETE

B. H. Babbage

Part of Babbage's difference engine built in 1833. The engine was begun in 1823 and abandoned in 1842. The abandonment was caused more by the inventor's inability to know when to stop improving and start building, than by any failing in accurate workmanship (as has been suggested).

The original Hollerith US census tabulator. The card reader is on the right of the working surface. Spring-loaded pins are pushed through any holes in the card presented, making contact with mercury below and thus actuating the counters.

A Hollerith card for an early Norwegian census. The symbols indicate occupational classifications.

engine was never finished and he died in 1871.

Working on a more modest scale, and with less publicity, the Swedes Edward and Pehr Georg Scheutz of Stockholm developed and built a successful difference engine, which was exhibited in Paris in 1855. It was based on Babbage's work but it was less ambitious; it printed out answers to eight decimal places. The prototype was acquired by the Dudley Observatory, Albany NY, where it was used for calculating astronomical tables.

Punched cards

Somewhat more successful, Herman Hollerith pursued the punched card idea in an attempt to speed up the statistical analysis of the 1890 US census. Such was the magnitude of the task that the analysis of the 1880 census had barely been completed when it was 1890, and time for the next census. There had to be something better than analysis by hand. Hollerith turned to punched cards, and built a card reader with a panel of counting dials. A card was fed in and 'scanned' by an array of pins over cups of mercury. If a pin passed through a hole, it made contact with the mercury and completed an electric circuit, triggering the appropriate dials on the machine. Hollerith's machine was thus the first practical punched card data processor, and analysis of the 1890 census was completed in the unbelievably short time of six weeks.

Hollerith left the Census Bureau and set up the Tabulating Machine Company in 1896; the demand for the machines was overwhelming. Out of it grew International Business Machines (IBM), and punched card systems for accounting and statistical analysis were used well into the 1960s and 70s – until, in fact, businesses changed over to full-scale computers.

The Comptometer

The Comptometer appeared in 1886. This was the invention of Dorr E Pett, a mechanic in the Pullman Company of Chicago. The Comptometer was a 'key-set' calculator with a typewriter-style keyboard which allowed numbers to be entered quickly. An important refinement to this invention appeared in 1892 when another American, William S Burroughs, patented a keyboard adder-lister which produced a printed record of what had been entered, plus a total at the end.

Now it was no longer necessary to employ people with a good head for figures. In time, some typewriters had an adding and subtracting mechanism fitted. Indeed, the book-keeping clerk was the office member whose future was most grievously affected by the electro-mechanical advances from now on. The Victorian male clerk, writing with quills and figuring in his head, was supplanted by a female clerk using a machine!

In office terms, calculating machines were a godsend; in mathematical terms offices didn't need to function at any more sophisticated a level. The road to computers, and eventually pocket calculators,

A Burroughs adding and listing machine. This machine produces lists of cheques, invoices, *etc* (keyed in by the operator) and prints them with sub-totals and totals.

A Burroughs non-listing adding machine. This machine is used for adding lists already entered in ledgers by hand.

Barrett Desk Electric

Designed and Built to Assure

**Accuracy and Durability
Quiet and Speedy Operation
Ten Column Total Capacity**

Electric
Model
91-E

$137

When you write for our Special Dealer Offer, we will send you the famous Monotype Souvenir—the Lord's Prayer cast complete on a type this size ☐ and a booklet describing it.

CAPACITY
99,999,999.99

BARRETT DIVISION

LANSTON MONOTYPE MACHINE COMPANY

Monotype Bldg., Twenty-fourth at Locust Street, Philadelphia, Pa.

Even in 1931 there were special offers to attract customers.

40

followed the need to solve highly complex mathematical problems such as the differential equations connected with ballistics, tidal and astronomical calculations.

The computer emerges

The mathematical path was that followed by Dr Vanevar Bush who, in the 1930s at the Massachusetts Institute of Technology, constructed a machine for solving differential equations – the Bush differential analyser. An unexpected importance of this machine was that it led to the Moore School of Electrical Engineering in Pennsylvania, and the universities of Cambridge and Manchester in Britain, becoming centres of excellence for post-war computer development.

The problem finally became one of the machines working faster than they could be fed, the solution to which would be an internal memory (the whole made possible by advances in solid-state electronics). The American John von Neumann was the first to describe in detail the concept of the stored-programme digital computer: a machine with a central control unit, a central processor and random access memory.

As time went on, business offices began to reap the benefits of military-motivated, government-financed mathematics programmes, and the great machines which were being built in the centres of excellence. In 1953 the British catering firm J Lyons & Co built a computer named LEO (Lyons electronic office) for the unheard-of purpose of electronic data processing.

Suddenly, everyone had heard of the 'electronic brain' which was capable of an amazing variety of tasks and which would change everyone's life. No one could deny that computers have changed our lives, but perhaps not in the ways predicted.

By the 1960s the speed and storage capacity of computers was proving itself to businesses whose paper storage systems were being sorely tried. Once installed, computers quickly became the primary office machine at least in big business: information was finding its own technology.

Left
The pocket calculator emerged in the 1970s, popularized and cleverly marketed by Sir Clive Sinclair.

In the 1970s, computers began to become more compact; smaller organizations could buy a 'minicomputer' as opposed to a 'mainframe'. Electronics manufacturing technology was developing rapidly, until millions of 'devices' could be packed on to one 'chip'. Throughout the 1980s and beyond, computers became smaller and smaller and more and more powerful, and it is a rare office today which has no computer – and many have one on every desk.

The technology has found its way into many other pieces of office equipment, from the photocopier to the postal scales. Computer technology has transformed the appearance of the office but the functions remain similar to those which an (intelligent) 15th or 16th century merchant's clerk would recognize.

The accounting and mathematics side of office work is but one side of the story. We end up in the same place however – a computer storage system – if we follow the writing side of clerking. For not only did clerks have to be able to add up and take away but they had to write legibly and have excellent memories.

Copying

Let us return to the 16th century when office work was increasing. In Tudor times merchants wrote their own letters. These were dated, numbered, sealed and copied twice: one for the record, and the other sent to guard against the possibility that the first might have got 'lost'.

To alleviate the tedium of all that copying, tinkerers and sometime inventors first turned their energies to means of making copies. In November 1655 there is an entry in John Evelyn's diary about his visit to the 'honest and learned Mr Hartlib', who told him of 'an ink that would give a dozen copies when moist sheets of paper were pressed on it: and gave me a recipe how to take off any print without the least injury to the original'.

There was no subsequent evidence as to this ink being further used, though the idea sounds similar to the one James Watt devised a century or so later.

A mechanical means of writing had been pursued since the end of the 17th century. In 1647 a patent was granted to William Petty for a machine which 'might be learnt in an hour's time and of great advantage to lawyers, scriveners, merchants, scholars, clerks etc.' In fact it turned out to be some sort of jointed mechanism attached to one pen so as to work another at the same time.

Another such machine, invented by Sir Marc Isambard Brunel (father of the more famous son) in 1799, is now in the Science Museum, London. A Mr Hawkins of Frankford, Philadelphia invented one which became much used by Thomas Jefferson: 'I think this is the finest invention of the present age'. These devices tended to be used more by individuals than in offices by clerks. There was still plenty of time, money and labour to handle office work.

Watt's patent

In 1780, as a result of the tedium of copying his lengthy correspondence with his Birmingham works, James Watt patented his 'invention of a new method of copying letters and other writing expeditiously'. The idea was as simple as could be. You write on good quality paper using a special copying ink. When the ink is dry, you press a thin moistened sheet of tissue paper firmly on it. The impression is a mirror image, but the paper is thin enough to read from the other side and therefore the right way round.

Watt marketed his machine and sold about 200 – too few, alas, to improve the lot of the clerk. In business circles copies, other than those made conventionally by hand, smacked of forgery. It was to take some years more before the pace of clerical work had speeded up sufficiently for the need for a mechanical copier to become self-evident.

Wedgwood's patent

Much the same suspicious reception was accorded the Stylographic Writer which Ralph Wedgwood (a member of a collateral branch of the pottery family) patented in 1806. An inked sheet of paper was dried and placed between two other sheets. An impression of the writing on the top copy was transferred to the underneath copy. The initial writing was done with a metal stylus to ensure a clear copy underneath, but if the top paper was thin enough the inked impression on its reverse side could be read from the right side. The bottom sheet was sent out and the thin top one retained.

The copying book

In the next 60 years or so the pace of clerical work in offices accelerated enormously in response to the rapid expansion of industry and trade. Discoveries of new processes and materials had effects in other areas. In the late 1850s a British chemist, William Perkin, discovered mauvine, the first aniline (synthetic) dye. This coincided with the first imports of Japanese paper which was strong, thin, and transparent, and responsive to the new strong aniline copying inks.

Watt's copying device came into its own in offices in the form of the letter-copying book. This was adopted as standard procedure in the 1870s and the copies it contained were accepted in courts of law. The letter copying book contained all the tissues ready to be dampened and pressed on to the original document using a copying press. The new inks made the process easier than in Watt's day and a skilful copier could work efficiently at great speed. Of course, only outgoing correspondence could be copied in this way; incoming documents still had to be copied by hand if copies were needed.

Carbon paper

Whereas the letter copying book was admissible in court, carbon copies were not. Wedgwood had referred to 'carbonated paper' in his invention, and some carbon copies of papers written by the Duke of Wellington in about 1809 have been found. Coating paper with lamp black and oil was a messy process and the result was no cleaner to use.

The process was in far more general use in America than in Britain. From 1823 carbon paper was made by Cyrus P Dakin of Concord, MA; he sold it exclusively to the Associated Press. In 1868 in Cincinatti the Associated Press was covering the balloon ascent of Lebbeus H Rogers, an intrepid aeronaut engaged in a celebration stunt for the biscuit and greengrocery firm of which he'd just been made partner on his 21st birthday. During his post-stunt interview, Rogers noticed the carbon paper and, ever watchful of an opportunity as befitted his recently elevated status, realized its useful application in copying office documents. He soared from biscuits to carbons in one stunt, going on to make a fortune from carbon paper.

Quill pens were not much good at providing the pressure needed to make a carbon copy. Metal pens were better but the machine most suited to carbon copying was the typewriter, as Lebbeus Rogers

This range of duplicating devices was available in the 1930s.

illustrated during a demonstration in 1872.

The number of readable copies which could be made with carbons was limited, although a sharp typewriter could produce, say, half a dozen or more of decreasing clarity (indicating the recipient's status). But businesses were expanding: customers needed to be circularized with details of newly available products, and banks, railway companies, insurance companies, estate agents, and new local government offices all had information to disseminate. What was really needed was a facility for unlimited copying.

The hectograph

The hectograph went some way to satisfying this need. With this device, the original to be copied was written in a special ink and placed face down on a layer of gelatine, on to which the ink image was transferred. Copies were made by laying fresh sheets of paper on the gelatine and gently smoothing them with a roller. The process was particularly messy and was closely associated with Perkin's new aniline inks, now largely made in Germany whence Perkin had emigrated.

The principle of the hectograph was mechanized into the spirit duplicator, or 'ditto machine', much used in schools in days of yore for producing almost illegible worksheets and internal examination papers in pale purple, green and pink. The image was transferred to the back of a master sheet by laying the master on another sheet of paper, whose surface colour was transferable, and writing on it. The master sheet was then fastened to the drum of the machine, and wiped with spirit from a felt pad as the drum was turned. Sheets of paper fed through received gradually deteriorating copies of the image

The stencil duplicator

As the wonder of the hectograph evaporated, inventors in America and Britain started to investigate making copies by means of stencilling. There was nothing particularly original in the idea; what was needed to make it work for duplicating was the combination of a suitable writing implement and suitable paper. In 1847 Eugenio de Zuccato, an Italian law student, patented an 'Improvement in producing facsimile copies of writing, drawings and delineations' – known as the Papyrograph.

The master sheet was coated with lacquer to prevent

The electric pen in use. It is powered by two wet cells which drive an off-balance rotor on top of the stylus, causing the stylus to vibrate and perforate the stencil.

ink passing into it, except where a steel nib wrote using a solution of caustic soda in place of ink. The soda softened the lacquer so that an impression of the writing was left, forming a porous stencil.

At the same time as Zuccato was developing this, Thomas Edison in America was developing his electric pen. He produced three patents in 1877 in which he referred to a perforating pen, a pneumatic stencil pen and a stencil pen. The basic device was simple – a pointed stylus used to write on strong paper which was held on a finely-grooved steel plate. The stylus perforated the paper with hundreds of minute holes.

Ink could then be pushed through the resulting stencil onto ordinary paper – making thousands of copies, it was claimed.

Edison's process met with great success in America; salesmen who visited Europe, however, came home dispirited at the lack of interest. For many, the special pen was a poorly-balanced writing implement and anyway was too much of an ingenious-looking curiosity wired up as it was to its two wet cells, to find acceptance.

Zuccato produced his next invention, the Trypograph, in 1877. This time, the paper was coated with paraffin wax, placed on a 'file plate', and written on with a blunt metal stylus. File plates were the result of common thinking in duplicating circles, the stylus needing a rough under-surface on which to write. Edison himself patented an idea based on a file plate, but did nothing about it commercially while he was marketing his electric pen.

In 1880 David Gestetner took out a British patent for an alternative plate built from fine, close-lying wires. The final breakthrough in stencil making came with Gestetner's wheel pen. This had a small toothed wheel mounted on a steel shaft at the end of a wooden holder, and the perforations it made in the paper gave excellent reproduction. To complement the process Gestetner developed a stencil material using fibrous Japanese kite tissue impregnated with wax.

Gestetner called his pen the Cyclostyle, but in time the whole process around it assumed that name. In America the process became known as 'mimeograph-

Label from within the lid of the Neo-Cyclostyle duplicating apparatus.

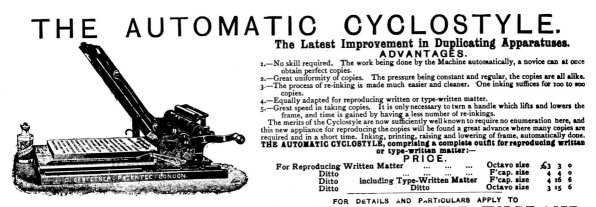

Above
An advertisement of 1885.

Left
An advertisement of 1889.

The Result of 25 years' experience in Duplicator Construction

Breuer's Patent
Multor-Automatic Model 46

The revolving duplicator with all technical perfections
at a reasonable price

Construction:

Completely made of special cast alloy; all parts are, therefore, 100 per cent. accurate. All parts with non-rusting nickel plating. Precision workmanship throughout.

Technical Features:

Simple and reliably working automatic paper feed with adjustable printing margin.

Automatic brush inking, preventing drying up of ink. Always clean hands.

All revolving parts running on hardened roller bearings, which ensure exceptionally smooth running.

Counter with instantaneous zero adjustment which can be stopped for trial prints.

1 Automatic Printing Margin Adjustment allows for accurate overprinting. Very important when printing forms.

2 Stop-Device prevents wrong turning of handle.

3 Automatic Brush-Inking distributes ink uniformly and economically by simple to-and-fro' movement of handle.

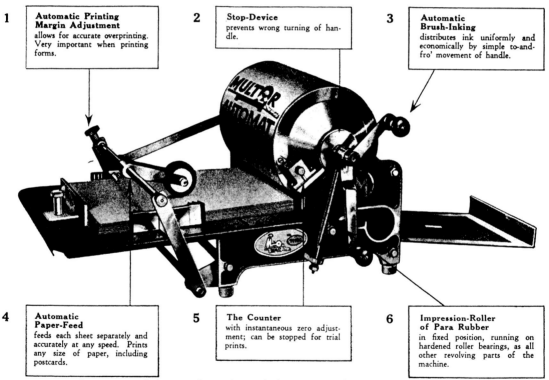

4 Automatic Paper-Feed feeds each sheet separately and accurately at any speed. Prints any size of paper, including postcards.

5 The Counter with instantaneous zero adjustment; can be stopped for trial prints.

6 Impression-Roller of Para Rubber in fixed position, running on hardened roller bearings, as all other revolving parts of the machine.

On account of the smooth running and the exceptionally ingenious and simple construction of the machine, everybody can operate it instantly with the greatest ease.

Write for our advantageous Dealer Terms!

MULTOR G.M.B.H.

Liberal Discounts and Turn-Over Bonuses.

BERLIN W. 30. - MOTZ-STR. 79 A.

For U. S. A. and Canada:
ELMER BREUER
320 Broadway, New York City.

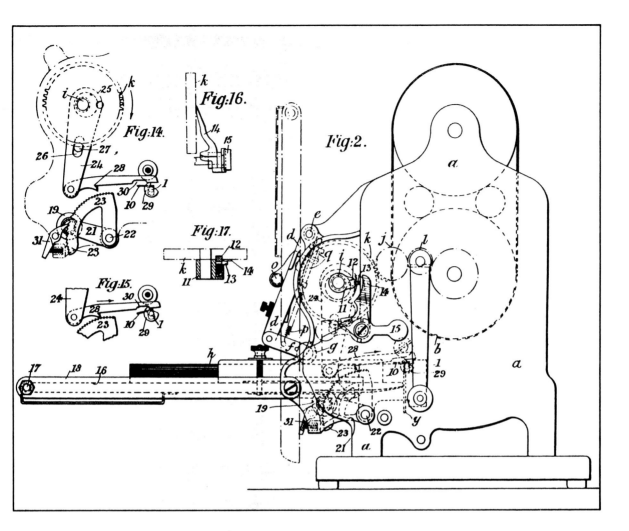

Figures labelled: Fig:14, Fig:15, Fig:16, Fig:17, Fig:2.

Gestetner's British patent no 18,257 of 1905. Instead of fitting round a drum, the stencil is mounted on a band passing round two rollers. The ink is distributed evenly on the main rollers by a pair of oscillating ink rollers, providing a quality of office reproduction which, it was suggested, could rival printing.

Left
Duplicators other than those of Gestetner continued to use the single drum.

ing' after A B Dick launched a file-plate stencil duplicator called the Mimeograph in 1887.

Gestetner refined his pen to make writing with it easy and comfortable. He called his new pen the Neocyclostyle (the American patent called it the Neostyle) and it was an instant success with those using it. In Britain it was somewhat harder to sell – there being neither 'style' nor 'elegance' in copies – but sell it did. He then moved on to developing a tissue – again from Japanese fibre – suitable for cutting typewritten stencils.

Having developed a satisfactory way of making the stencils, Gestetner turned his attention to mechanizing the printing process. In 1891 he acquired a patent for his Automatic Cyclostyle duplicating apparatus, of which an important aspect was the means of spreading the ink so that it squeezed through the stencil evenly.

The powered version of the Victoria automatic rapid letter copier (*ca* 1906) could produce a photographic copy in three seconds.

Gestetner's rotary duplicator – the Rotary Cyclostyle – subsequently had two rollers over which the fabric carrier and its stencil passed, and remained a faithful servant in offices from the early years of the century until the 1970s or 80s as photocopiers took over.

In America the single drum rotary duplicator held sway. Roneo was a rival company started by a relation of Gestetner, and took its name from Gestetner's Rotary Neostyle.

The photocopier

The stencil duplicator is fine when the user is the originator of the document, but less useful when incoming documents are to be copied. The photocopier dates from 1907, and has always been most suited to that task, though early photocopiers were messy and smelly, and needed special papers and chemical solutions. They developed as far as they could, but the answer to the need lay in xerography – dry writing.

In xerography, an image of the matter to be copied is focused on to an electrostatically-charged, light-sensitive surface. The charge remains on the image, and attracts a black powder, which is then transferred to ordinary paper and fixed by means of heat. The process was invented by Chester F Carlson in 1937, but was turned down by a score of companies to whom he offered it. At last – in 1944 – Carlson obtained financial support from the Batelle Memorial Institute, working on the invention until the Haloid Company of Rochester, NY acquired the patent rights in 1950. There was a tremendous amount of further development needed, but Carlson's tenacity won – as a look round any modern office and the term 'xerox' will testify.

The filing system

Organizing the increasing mounds of paper became a fundamental task in offices. It seemed that the new mechanical processes – typewriting and copying – were no more than means of breeding paper exponentially.

The spike had long been an adequate filing system for most businesses, but the increasing rate at which paper came in began to defeat the recall powers of even the most photographic of memories. Files began to appear in the mid-19th century: concertina, vertical, box, horizontal and in cabinets. By the early years of

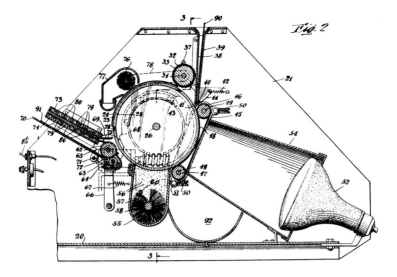

An illustration of the xerographic process from British patent no 679,533 of 1952. The original American application was filed by Chester F Carlson in 1940. The illuminated image is focused on the surface of the light-sensitive drum 25, leaving an electrical charge on the surface of the drum, corresponding to the image it has 'seen'. The charge attracts a black powder 56, which is transferred from the surface of the drum to the paper for the copy. The image is then fixed on the paper by heat.

the 20th century, it was apparent that storage was going to become daunting. Filing clerks had to be employed simply to make sure that everything was where it should be and easily found if required.

This is where we meet up again with the storage capacity of office computers. Copies of outgoing and incoming correspondence and information can all be stored, ready for processing at the flick of a disk – indeed, correspondence can be sent from one computer to another without need of paper. The computer has become the ultimate artificial total recall memory which will analyse on demand – several steps away from even the most efficient and skilled of Victorian clerks. We are working towards the 'paperless office', where all records are stored in computer memory, or transferred therefrom to magnetic tape or compact disks, one of which will hold the equivalent of several filing cabinets full of paper. Information is transferred from one person to another via the computer network, and read on the screen. However, it will take some time for people to get used to working in this way, and the

facility for referring to several documents at once will need some thought.

In the late 1940s and early 1950s 'low tech' aids began to pour into offices. According to *White Collar:*

There is a mechanical collator whose metal fingers snatch sheets of paper from five piles in proper sequence and staple them for distribution. There are ticket and money counters, mechanical erasers, automatic signature machines which promise office production from 25 to 300 per cent. Gadgets can add, subtract, multiply, divide and duplicate all at once; can type in fifty-one languages, open and seal envelopes, stamp and address them. There is a billing machine that takes raw paper in at one end, cuts it to size, perforates it, prints two-color forms on it, prints the amounts of the bills, addresses them and neatly piles them up for the postman. There is an incredibly dextrous machine into which cards are slipped which sends out tailor-made replies to every imaginable complaint and inquiry.

If we think back to the offices of Scrooge, Pooter and Smeeth, the striking difference lies in the numbers of people operating clerical machines – just like a factory.

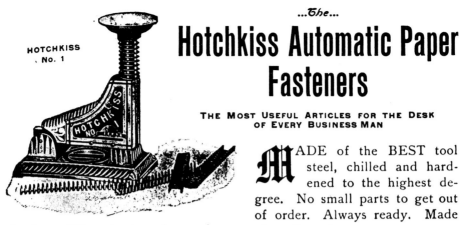

HOTCHKISS
No. 1

...The...
Hotchkiss Automatic Paper Fasteners

THE MOST USEFUL ARTICLES FOR THE DESK OF EVERY BUSINESS MAN

MADE of the BEST tool steel, chilled and hardened to the highest degree. No small parts to get out of order. Always ready. Made in four different sizes for various grades of work.

No. 1 as shown in illustration uses a single strip of 25 staples which are fed forward and cut off automatically. The staple is always ready to be driven and a single sharp blow will put together anywhere from 2 to 25 sheets of ordinary paper,

No. 2 is a larger and heavier machine with a lever attachment and is more suitable for heavy work, having a stapling capacity of 50 sheets or over.

No. 3 is the largest of the four machines and has more than double the capacity of the number one. It is not so large, however, but that it can be used on the desk.

HOTCHKISS
No. 4

No. 4 as shown in illustration is a new machine just placed on the market. It uses a strip of 50 staples instead of the usual 25 as in the other machines and has a straight carrier at the back which protects the entire strip of staples.

The Automatic Tag Machine

The BEST machine on the market for putting tags or shipping cards on boxes, barrels, crates, cars, etc. It drives a staple or double tack into the hardest wood or through tin. It can be used for putting paper on the wall where tacks are used, being neat and accurate. The machine is absolutely perfect and cannot get out of order. Don't pound your fingers and waste time hunting for tacks and hammer when the "Automatic" is always ready.

1,000 STAPLES FURNISHED WITH EVERY MACHINE SOLD EITHER FOR THE PAPER FASTENERS OR TAG MACHINES

Extra Staples Always In Stock Ready to be Shipped Immediately. For further Information, Catalog and Prices, address

Alex. H. Irvin Company
(INCORPORATED)

Sole Dealers for the United States and Foreign Countries Curwensville, Penn., U.S.A.

Staples were available for everything from paper to cars!

The 'Protectograph' cheque writer, a forgery protection device exhibited at Cardiff in 1923.

The Rockwell-Watson superior vertical filing system. It appears that, at the turn of the century, the protruding tabs on the cards facilitating information retrieval were a breakthrough.

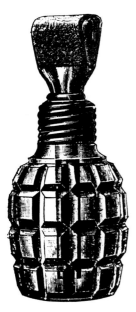

Mr J Funnell Christian's capillary stamp and envelope moistener (1891). This 'capital article' will be 'sure to command a large sale.'

The authoritative Automatic Time Stamp of about 1900 subdivides the business day into minutes and its imprint 'fixes the responsibility for negligence or delay beyond question or argument.'

An office might be described as an information exchange: information comes in, information goes out.

Lack of sophisticated means of transmitting information has never hindered trade and commerce. Well-tramped routes had their own couriers and messengers. In medieval times, these were Papal envoys, monks, pilgrims or representatives of kings and ducal houses. Confidentiality couldn't always be ensured of course, nor safe delivery, and sometimes it was better to send a private emissary. But the 'system' worked and trade certainly expanded.

The port of Dover grew up because it was from there that Royal envoys sailed. This service was subsequently used by merchants; London to Calais was only two days, significantly quicker than to most places inland. By Tudor times there were regular services to Spain, Antwerp, Calais and Bordeaux.

The post

The British Post Office dates from 1635 when King Charles I found that money could be made from the royal postal service. Dates of posting were stamped on letters and the cost of postage was assessed by the number of sheets of paper making up the letter. Originally, the system of 'posts' – the men whose job it was to carry the mail – did not operate in London. Accordingly, in 1680, a merchant named William Docwra organized his own penny post. The scheme was so successful that the government closed it down (!) on the grounds that it infringed the King's monopoly – promptly reopening it for its own benefit. It was a receiver-to-pay service, but it declined in profitability because so many of the classes of people who used the service – peers, state officials, members of parliament – had 'franking' privileges, that is to say they were exempt from payment. Roland Hill's penny post of 1840 reversed that and, without exception, the sender of a letter had to pay before it was accepted.

Envelopes as we know them date from this time. There is evidence of a Babylonian form of clay envelope and mention was made in contemporary literature of a letter sent by the Duke of Saxe Gotha in 1640 which was folded envelope-style. Jonathan Swift (1667–1746) used the word 'envelope' in 1735 but probably meant a paper sleeve. From 1840 envelopes could be purchased complete with stamps – the 'Mulready' envelope. Mulreadies were commonly derided and before long were withdrawn. Senders then had to affix their own stamps to their own envelopes in the position dictated by the Post Office.

Before sealed envelopes, letters were folded and a blob of melted wax dropped on the join. A seal was sometimes pressed on to the wax leaving imprints of initials, mottoes, messages, coats of arms etc. This is the origin of the signet ring.

Various machines appeared towards the end of the 19th century to ease the load of the clerks handling the outgoing mail – machines for sealing, addressing and stamping envelopes. Addressing machines worked by hand or treadle and produced stencilled or typographed addresses, the individual type being set in small frames.

The idea of a postage meter or 'franking machine' interested an American, Arthur H Pitney, about the turn of the century when he realised how easy it was for office boys to help themselves to the office stamps. The American postal authorities needed some persuading that a business could be responsible for its own franking. The machine Pitney developed with an Englishman, Walter Bowes, was finally accepted by the post offices in America in 1920 and in Britain in 1922.

The telegraph

The need for communicating more quickly than by letter or messenger became apparent in the early days

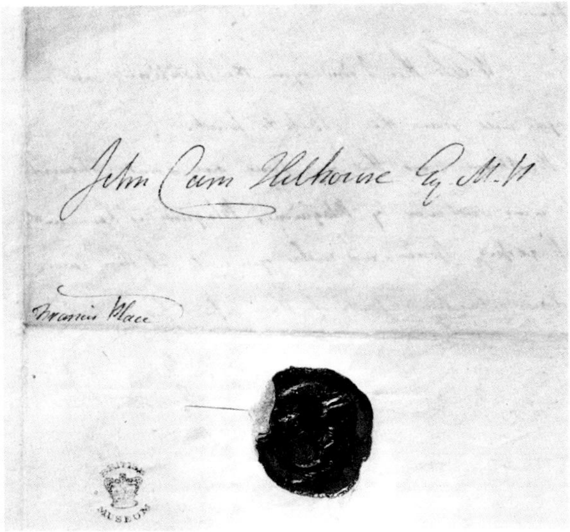

Above

Before sealed envelopes, letters were folded and a blob of melted wax dropped on the join. A seal was sometimes pressed on to the wax leaving imprints of initials, mottoes, messages, coats of arms *etc.*

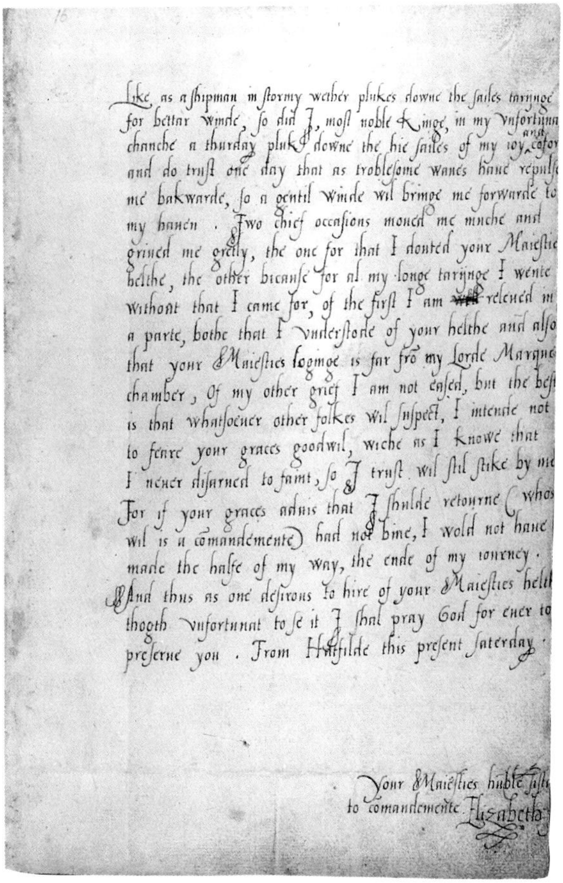

Right

A letter from Princess Elizabeth to King Edward VI, ripe with nautical metaphor.

A Mulready cover (1840) showing an allegorical representation of Britannia sending out messages all over the world by means of elephants *etc.* Mulreadies were ridiculed out of existence.

The handwritten letter reads:

Like as a shipman in stormy weather plukes downe the sailes taryinge for bettar winde, so did I, most noble Kinge, in my vnfortunat chaunche a thursday pluke downe the hie sailes of my ioy, and do trust one day that as troublesome wanes haue repulsed me bakwarde, so a gentil winde wil bringe me forwarde to my hauen. Two chief occasions mouch me muche and grieud me gretly, the one for that I donted your Maiesties helthe, the other becanse for al my longe taryinge I wente without that I came for, of the first I am relieued in a parte, bothe that I vnderstode of your helthe and also that your Maiesties loginge is far fro my Lorde Marques chamber, Of my other grief I am not eased, but the best is that whatsoeuer other folkes wil suspect, I intende not to fence your graces goodwil, wiche as I knowe that I neuer disarued to faint, so I trust wil stil stike by me. For if your graces aduis that I shulde retourne (whos wil is a comandemente) had not bine, I wold not haue made the halfe of my way, the ende of my iourney. And thus as one desirous to hire of your Maiesties helth thoogh vnfortunat to se it I shal pray God for euer to preserue you. From Hatfilde this present saterday.

Your Maiesties humble sister to comandemente Elizabeth

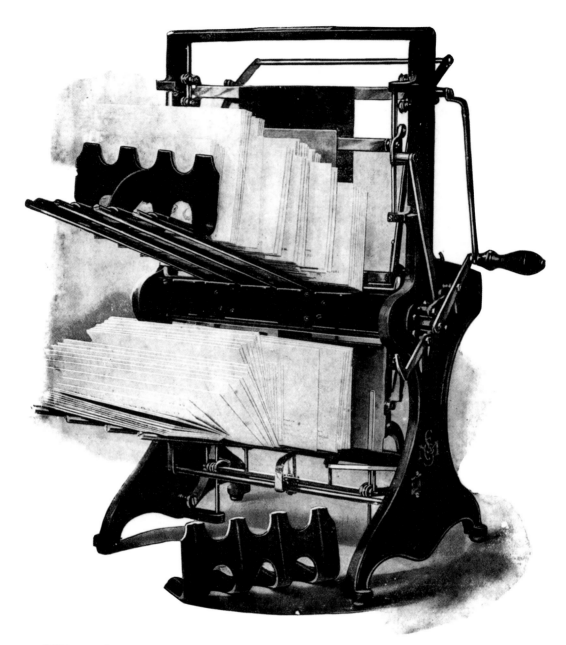

The Simplex Automatic Envelope Sealer

(Hand power).   Height 21 in.   Base 12 in. × 13½ in

Showing an assortment of envelopes with various enclosures being put through the machine.
The "follower" is removed from the lower rack as the envelopes themselves form sufficient
weight to compress flaps while drying.

**The only machine that will seal your letters and guarantee
to keep them sealed.**

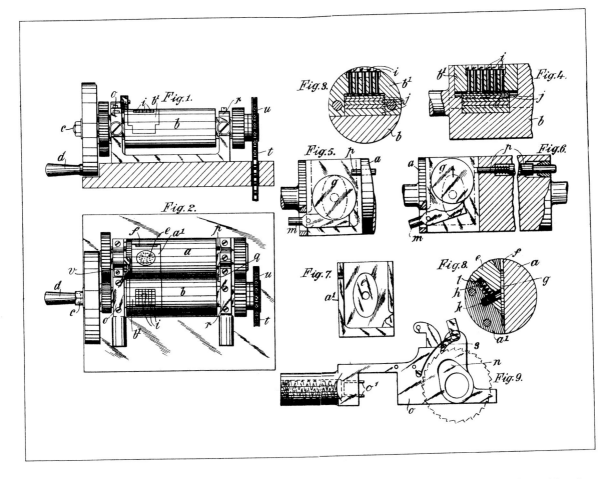

Wilkinson's British patent no 17,707 of 1911 for a postal franking machine. The impression rollers are seen in Figure 2.

of the railways; something that would travel faster than a train was needed.

In 1753, someone writing as 'CM' in the *Scots Magazine* suggested that messages might be sent down wires by electricity – one wire for each letter of the alphabet. This apparatus would have had to have used 'static' electricity, generated with a friction machine, since current electricity (generated by batteries) was undiscovered. The apparatus would have been incredibly slow and clumsy.

Things became easier when the electric 'battery' was invented; it was discovered that the electric current decomposes water into bubbles of oxygen and hydrogen. ST von Soemmering invented a system for sending messages in the form of bubbles released by electricity, but devices using this principle needed about 40 connecting wires, and were as slow and cumbersome as CM's apparatus would have been.

In 1832 a German diplomat, Baron Schilling, demonstrated a means of sending messages with a machine called a 'telegraph', using five magnetic needles. Had Schilling not died, he might have installed a system for the Csar Nicholas of Russia in 1836. In that same year, William Fothergill Cooke (1808–79) saw Schilling's telegraph, and was so inspired that he determined to invent a system of his own.

Cooke's first telegraph had three circuits, each with a pair of wires connected to a sensitive device (galvanometer) to detect the current at the receiving end. Reversing the current in a circuit reversed the deflection of the galvanometer needle. However, Cooke ran into difficulties so he sought help from Charles

Wheatstone (1802–75), professor of natural philosophy at King's College, London.

Wheatstone was already working on telegraphy, so he and Cooke decided to join forces. They took out their first patent – for a five-needle telegraph – in 1837. Each circuit terminates in a pair of coils which makes an associated needle swing one way or the other, according to the direction in which the current flows in the circuit. Letters on the diamond-shaped face are identified by pointing two needles at them. This gives 20 combinations; letters C, J, Q, U, X and Z are missing.

If one of the 20 positions on the Wheatstone & Cooke telegraph had been designated a 'shift key', the five-needle telegraph could have transmitted 38 characters – for example 26 letters, 10 digits and two punctuators.

As the railways spread across Britain from 1830 onwards, there was a growing need for communications between stations, partly in the interest of safety. The railways also had a profound effect on time: once each community had its own time, based on the local public clock. The railways introduced a standard 'railway time', and were able to synchronise their clocks via the telegraph.

In 1838, Wheatstone and Cooke installed a 20km (13 mile) telegraph line from the London district of Paddington to West Drayton on the Great Western Railway. The demonstration was so successful that they extended the telegraph to Slough in 1842. By this time, they were using a double-needle telegraph, each needle controlled by a three-position handle. Including the rest position (both vertical) two three-position needles have nine combinations. The code for the whole alphabet was therefore somewhat complex, and transmission was slow. Nevertheless, the railways installed many two-needle instruments and many miles of telegraph wire in the first few years of the 1840s.

The telegraph came to the notice of the public in 1845, when one John Tawell murdered a woman named Hart at Salthill, and fled on the train from Slough to London. As he looked out of the window, little did he know that his description was being flashed along those telegraph wires. When he arrived in London, he was arrested, and in due course tried, found guilty, and hanged.

Some time later, a group of people, all strangers to one another, travelled from Slough to London by train. They sat in silence, as people on English trains always

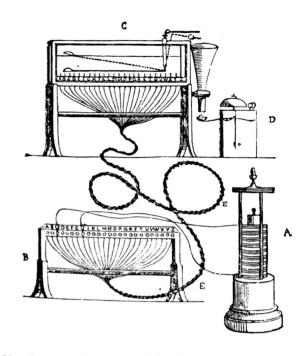

Von Soemmering's electrolytic telegraph has a separate wire for each character. When the voltaic pile A is connected to a chosen character, the bell D rings at the receiving station, and bubbles in the receiving tank indicate the characters transmitted.

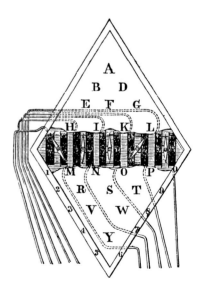

The workings of the five-needle telegraph. Electromagnets deflect pairs of needles so that they point to chosen letters on the diamond-shaped display.

have done, when a man, who was looking out of the window, suddenly pointed at the telegraph wires and exclaimed in awe: 'Them's the cords that hung John Tawell!'

Samuel F B Morse (1791–1872) was an artist (and the first professor of the literature of art and design at New York University) who became enthusiastic about the idea of building an electric telegraph during a sea voyage in 1832. Morse had the idea of sending pulses of current which would energize an electromagnet, pressing a pen down to mark a moving strip of paper.

Morse's original idea for transmitting the electrical pulses was to have little blocks carrying raised studs, with a unique pattern for each letter of the alphabet, and the numerals. The blocks to make up a message would be assembled in a carrier – or 'rule' – and pulled past a contact operated by the studs on the blocks. Morse called the device for carrying the rule the 'port rule'.

Morse seemed to have something against the hand-operated key, and devised a tablet of ivory with conducting inlays so that the operator could draw a contact across the surface to generate impulses corresponding to the characters to be sent. When Morse finally acknowledged the possibility of using a switch or 'key', it started as a somewhat cumbersome affair.

The telegraph operators themselves soon developed skills of sending and receiving Morse would scarcely have dreamed of. Hand-keyed transmissions of 175 symbols a minute have been recorded; receiving at over 1,000 symbols a minute has also been achieved.

It is no coincidence that Thomas Edison's first job was as a telegraph operator with Western Union and that a large number of his patents had some connection with varying aspects of communication of sound. The early days of telegraph were exciting times and to a person of Edison's inventiveness all sorts of problems and refinements presented themselves and demanded solutions. He spent much of this early part of his working life reading scientific journals and fooling his supervisors into thinking he was at his post (and not asleep, which commonly happened to telegraph operators) by rigging his receiver to respond with the appropriate call sign. Although most people could be caught out once too often, Edison proved too valuable an asset to be dismissed. He also had a sound commercial sense.

A classical two-needle telegraph. The signalling bell is housed at the top; the sending handles are at the base of the cabinet. 'A boy will after a few weeks' practice learn to read the signals and to transmit messages with considerable rapidity.'

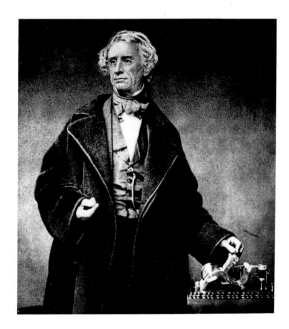

Professor Samuel Finley Breese Morse (1791-1872).

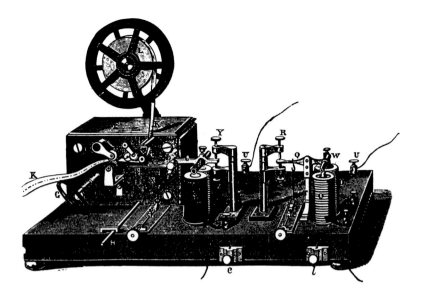

Left

The signals received by the Morse receiving instrument may be very feeble, so the incoming wires are connected to a coil which attracts an armature when it is energized. This is the 'relay' (right), so called because it 'hands on' the effect of the incoming signal like a runner's baton. The relay actuates the electromagnetic coils in the centre of the board, which pull an inked disk against a paper strip, fed from the reel by clockwork in the box under the reel. When the device receives pulses of current, they are printed as dots or dashes – Morse code – on the strip.

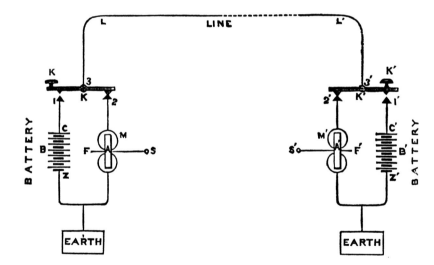

Right

Comprehensive diagrams in Alexander Graham Bell's British patent no 4,765 of 1876 for a telephone. Figure 19 shows the transmit/receive mouthpiece/earpieces with their magneto-electric coils.

Earth return telegraph circuit. It was soon discovered that there was no need for two wires to complete the circuit. Conducting plates buried in the ground at each station would provide an 'earth return'. The diagram shows two stations, each of which can act as either transmitter or receiver. Depressing the Morse key at one station connects its battery, and sends a current to the relay at the other station.

MORGAN-BROWN'S PROVISIONAL SPECIFICATION.

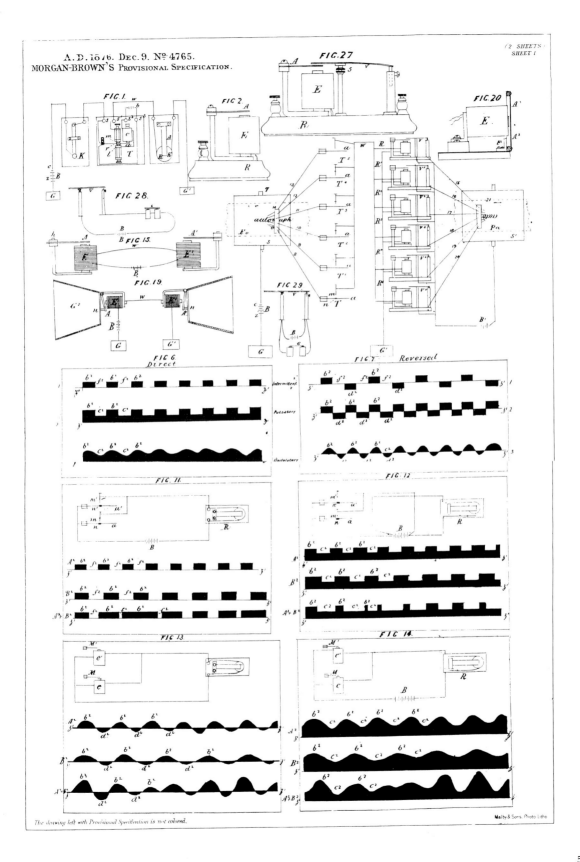

The drawing left with Provisional Specification is not colored.

Alexander Graham Bell inaugurating the New York – Chicago telephone line in 1892.

A view of the corner of Broadway and John Street, New York, in 1890. Replacing the overhead wires with underground cables improved the cityscape immensely.

The telephone

Both Edison and the Scotsman Alexander Graham Bell have been credited with 'inventing' the telephone. In fact the underlying principles were common at the time and a logical extension of principles embodied in the telegraph. In the event each contributed complementary ideas to the ultimate instrument.

Bell realised that if vibrations of sound waves could be transformed into a fluctuating electric current it should be possible to turn the fluctuations back into sound waves. He was the first person to transmit recognizable speech through wires, in 1876 in Boston, Massachusetts, where he was then living. He patented his device the same year. That same year also, Edison sent a notice to the US Patent Office saying he was working on a similar idea.

In Bell's system the human voice generated only a weak electric current which was transmitted along the wire linking one instrument with the other. With Edison's, the human voice opened or closed a valve which regulated a current of any desired strength. Thus the transmitting distance was much greater. Nevertheless, Bell's receiver was far superior to Edison's. A certain inevitable rivalry between the two men was not resolved until 1880 in Britain, whence Bell had returned in 1877 to publicize his invention. The British government had between 1868 and 1869 taken over all private telegraph companies and in 1879 decided that the telephone counted as a telegraph. The consequence was that private telephone companies – and both Bell and Edison had quickly established their own – would need an operating licence. The following year the two companies amalgamated to form the United (later National) Telephone Company and took out a 30-year licence.

From this time in Britain both the Post Office and the National Telephone Company established new exchanges – the Post Office tended to take care of small towns and rural areas; the National Telephone

Company larger towns. London was conveniently served by both systems and advertisements of the time often show two telephone numbers – if you couldn't get through on one then try the other.

'Singing and Talking by Telegraph' was the title of an article in *Chambers' Journal* of August 25 1877:

People are already ... acquainted ... with what is called the Telephone, or instrument for transmitting musical sounds to a distance ... But talking by electricity conveying the actual sounds of the voice for many miles – what are we to make of this?

Mr Elisha Gray appears to have made a definite advance. He has transmitted the piano sounds of a concert through the wire of an electric telegraph. The performer played at Philadelphia to an audience at New York, ninety miles distant.

This article is interesting on several counts. The original understanding by the writer – therefore his audience – of the concept of a telephone is obviously different from our own and the emphasis on the entertainment element makes us think of radio rather than telephone. Clearly the public needed a little time to digest the new device.

However, letters appeared in *The Times* before 1880 considering telephonic links a mixed blessing – certainly there was a reduction in travelling which would ease traffic congestion but, on the other hand, anyone could be disturbed at a caller's whim. Correspondents clearly foresaw the danger of intrusion from assiduous 'investment consultants', 'kitchen consultants','double-glazing consultants' and the rest.

The telephone had enormous implications for businesses of every kind. It wasn't simply that one could no longer hide behind a 'lost' letter: a wholly new dimension of speed of communication was introduced. Things ordered by 'phone could be dispatched more quickly; information passed by 'phone could be acted upon more quickly than if a correspondence had to be set up. The pace and order of the office day was 'interrupted' by 'demands' made by the telephone.

The spread of the telephone was much, much quicker in America than in Britain, as befitted an expanding and less entrenched society. The telephone did not become commonplace in British households until early in the 1960s.

Advertisement from a British Industries Fair catalogue of 1931.

The teleprinter

In the 1880s Edison gave some thought to a device which would record messages coming in by telegraph or telephone. The idea was to come to fruition as the teleprinter. Teleprinters communicate with each other rather like telephones except that the message is typed 'down the wire'. A copy of the message appears at the receiving end automatically. The teleprinter is less disturbing than the telephone, and has the advantage of producing 'hard copy' which somehow inspires action. Teleprinters have a worldwide network of their own called Telex (from *tele*printer *ex*change).

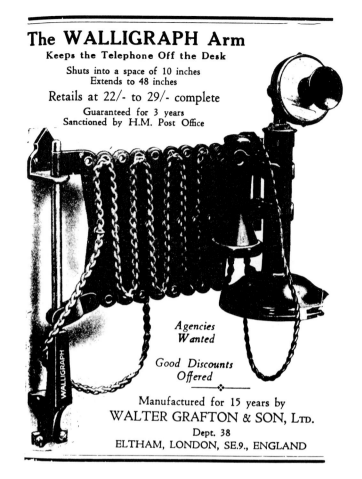

The WALLIGRAPH Arm

Keeps the Telephone Off the Desk

Shuts into a space of 10 inches
Extends to 48 inches

Retails at 22/- to 29/- complete

Guaranteed for 3 years
Sanctioned by H.M. Post Office

*Agencies
Wanted*

*Good Discounts
Offered*

Manufactured for 15 years by

WALTER GRAFTON & SON, Ltd.

Dept. 38
ELTHAM, LONDON, SE.9., ENGLAND

A space saver of 1931.

The fax

The teleprinter has the disadvantage that it can transmit and receive typed messages only. Much more versatile is the facsimile machine or 'fax', first described by the Scottish inventor Alexander Bain in his patent of 1841.

Bain used a paper which blackened when acted upon by an electric current, and 'scanned' both the image to be transmitted, and the receiving paper, synchronously. An electric current flowed when the scanner saw a dark part of the image, which reproduced that darkness on the receiving paper.

Bain's principles were developed until, by the 1920s, it was standard newspaper practice to send pictures 'by wire'.

The problem had always been to synchronize the transmitter and the receiver: equipment was slow and expensive. Everything changed when the image was 'digitized' – broken into elements which were either light or dark. The modern fax machine is inexpensive, reliable, rapid and of ever-better quality. Nowadays, few businesses of any size are without at least one fax machine, and the equipment is even finding its way into the home.

Envoi

As we leave the office with its myriad machines talking to one another without the need for human intervention, let us think on a sentence from *The Twentieth Century*: 'Rapid communications have corrupted good manners; for the speed with which people can travel or transmit news has aroused a nervous impatience of delay which is fatal to courtesy and good manners.' Perhaps this was written before we were used to 'modern life' as it then seemed. On balance, we think that the office is a great deal more demanding and exciting for its occupants than it was 100 years ago.

Chronology

Further reading

Michael Adler
The Writing Machine
Allen & Unwin 1973

W A Beeching
Century of the Typewriter
Heinemann 1976

H M Boettinger
The Telephone Book,
Bell, Watson, Vail and American Life Stearns 1983

M M Brownler
Women in the American Economy 1675–1929
Yale University Press 1976

Alice R Burks and Arthur Burks
The First Electronic Computer: The Atanasoff Story
Ann Arbor, University of Michigan Press 1988

H Casson
History of the Telephone
New York, Ayer 1977

R W Clark
Edison: The man who made the future
Macdonald & James London 1977

Rodney Dale
The Sinclair Story
Duckworth & Co 1985

Rodney Dale and
Ian Williamson
The Myth of the Micro
W H Allen 1980

Alan Delgado
The Enormous File
John Murray 1979

Charles Dickens
A Christmas Carol

Charles Dickens
Sketches by Boz

Carles Eames
A Computer Perspective
Cambridge, Harvard University Press 1973

Andrew Emmerson
Old Telephones
Shire Publications 1986

Mark Greenia
A History of Computing
Lexikon 1992

George and Weedon Grossmith
Diary of a Nobody
Many, 1892 on

Lee Holcombe
Victorian Ladies at Work
David & Charles 1973

Sinclair Lewis
The Job
1916

Michael Lindgren
Glory and Failure
MIT Press 1990

Peter C Marzio
The Man & Machines of American Journalism
Washington; Smithsonian Institution 1973

George Mell
Writing Antiques
Shire Publications 1980

C Wright Mills
White Collar: the American Middle Classes
OUP New York 1956

Barry Paine
Eliza Stories
Pavilion Books 1984

John Dos Passos
USA
1930

J B Priestly
Angel Pavement
Heinemann 1930

W B Proudfoot
The Origin of Stencil Duplicating
Hutchinson 1972

F J Romano
Machine Writing & Typesetting
1986

Silvanus P Thompson
Philipp Reis, Inventor of the Telephone
New York, Arno Press 1974

Geoffrey Tweedale
Calculating machines & Computers
Shire Publications 1990

A P Usher
History of Mechanical Inventions
Harvard University Press 1954

Van Waterford
All About Telephones
1983

Index

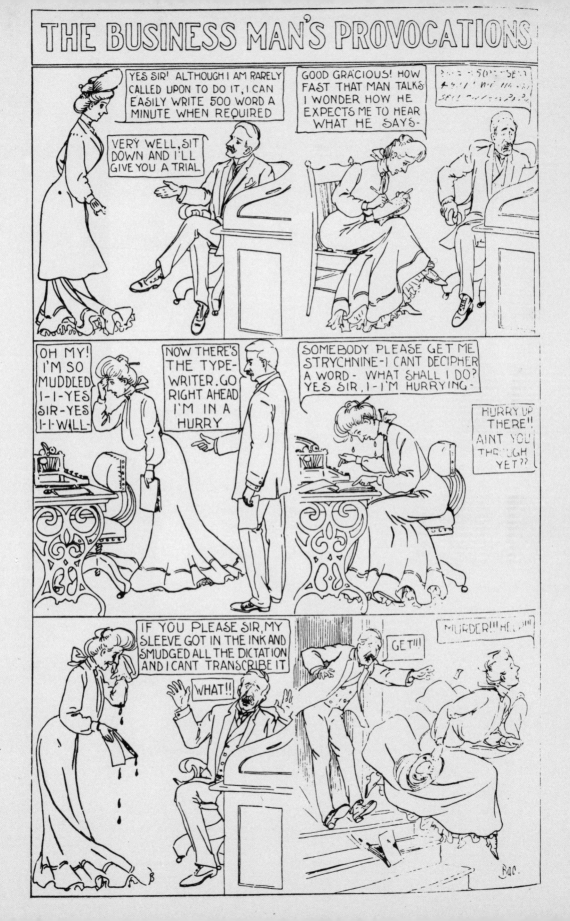